Betty Crocker's

RED SPOON COLLECTION™

BEST RECIPES FOR
PASTA

PRENTICE HALL

New York London Toronto Sydney Tokyo Singapore

Prentice Hall
15 Columbus Circle
New York, New York 10023

Published simultaneously in Canada by Prentice Hall Canada Inc.

Library of Congress Cataloging-in-Publication Data

Best recipes for pasta.—1st ed.
    p. cm.—(Betty Crocker's Red Spoon collection)
Includes index.
    1. Cookery (Pasta) I. Series
TX809.M17B46 1990
641.8′22—dc20   89-8424
                                       CIP

Manufactured in the United States of America

10 9 8 7 6 5 4 3 2 1

First Prentice Hall Edition

Front cover: Ravioli in Tomato Sauce

CONTENTS

INTRODUCTION

The popular success of pasta seems a recent phenomenon, but pasta is not new. In its many forms, pasta has been enjoyed around the world for centuries. Often based on grain ground into flour or meal, pasta has come to mean strands, sheets or small shapes of dough usually cooked by boiling. Pasta as a category embraces rice sticks and *wontons* from the Orient, Russian *pelmeni*, Armenian *monti* and Eastern European *kreplach* (all similar to Italian *ravioli*), the Japanese buckwheat noodles called *soba*, Asian mung bean noodles called "cellophane noodles" or "bean threads," and many variations besides.

Pasta can be astonishingly simple to prepare. Because it is such a nutritious food and stores so well in its dried form, it is the ideal kitchen cupboard staple. Properly cooked pasta is delicious simply tossed with butter and seasoned with salt and freshly ground pepper (refer to Red Spoon Tips, page 97, for hints on cooking pasta perfectly). A good number of traditional Italian pasta shapes have always been manufactured commercially—wheels and shells, for example—and although you are limited to making the simpler shapes at home, the reward for making fresh pasta is exceptional flavor and texture. Homemade pasta may not be as difficult to prepare as it appears. It is about as easy as making a pie crust, and after two or three tries, anyone can turn out fresh noodles with some skill. Refer to "Homemade Pasta and Versatile Sauces" (page 78) for the best of the fresh.

Making pasta at home doesn't call for a lot of fancy, expensive equipment. You can get by with a rolling pin and a sharp knife! For an introduction to some special pasta-making equipment available today, turn to pages 102–103.

Confused by the tremendous range of pasta shapes and sizes? The specific shapes are often made for specific uses. Some shapes are made for stuffing—the large shells, for example. Some are made especially for adding to soups; anelli, for example, and where would alphabet soup be without tiny pasta alphabet letters? Turn to our guide on pages 98–100 for help in choosing your pasta shapes.

Pasta has never been more popular with Americans than it is today. In addition to the proliferation of Italian restaurants, the pasta boom has gone on to spawn Japanese fast-food noodle shops and Chinese dumpling houses. Children seem to adore pasta—just go easy on the spicier seasonings like red pepper flakes, chili oil and the like—with spaghetti the perennial favorite. Many pasta dishes can be assembled, then frozen, for the do-ahead convenience that makes preparing food for a family so much easier.

We hope that you enjoy the opportunity this book gives you to try many of the delicious ways pasta is prepared around the world. From the simple to the sophisticated, there is something wonderful on the following pages for every taste under the sun.

· 1 ·

PASTA AND SOUP

Chicken Noodle Soup

Chicken and Broth (below)
2 medium carrots, sliced (about 1 cup)
2 medium stalks celery, sliced (about
* 1 cup)*
1 small onion, chopped (about ¼ cup)
1 tablespoon instant chicken bouillon
1 cup uncooked medium noodles (about
* 2 ounces)*

Prepare Chicken and Broth; reserve cut-up chicken. Add enough water to broth to measure 5 cups. Heat broth, carrots, celery, onion and bouillon (dry) to boiling; reduce heat. Cover; simmer until carrots are tender, about 15 minutes. Stir in noodles and chicken. Heat to boiling; reduce heat. Simmer uncovered until noodles are done, 7 to 10 minutes. Sprinkle with parsley, if desired.

CHICKEN AND BROTH

3- to 3½-pound broiler-fryer chicken,
* cut up*
4½ cups cold water
1½ teaspoons salt
½ teaspoon pepper
1 stalk celery with leaves, cut up
1 medium carrot, cut up
1 small onion, cut up
1 sprig parsley

Remove any excess fat from chicken. Place chicken, giblets (except liver) and neck in Dutch oven. Add remaining ingredients; heat to boiling. Skim foam; reduce heat. Cover and simmer until thickest pieces of chicken are done, about 45 minutes.

Remove chicken from broth; cool chicken just until cool enough to handle, about 10 minutes. Strain broth through cheesecloth-lined sieve. Remove chicken from bones and skin; cut up chicken. Discard bones, skin and vegetables. Skim fat from broth.

Chicken Soup with Tortellini

3- to 4-pound broiler-fryer chicken, cut
  up
6 cups water
1 stalk celery (with leaves), cut into 1-inch
  pieces
1 carrot, cut into 1-inch pieces
1 medium onion, cut into fourths
2 sprigs parsley
1 bay leaf
2½ teaspoons salt
1 teaspoon peppercorns
Tortellini (below)
2 cups water
Snipped fresh parsley
Grated Parmesan cheese

Heat chicken, 6 cups water, celery, carrot, onion, 2 sprigs parsley, bay leaf, salt and peppercorns to boiling in Dutch oven; reduce heat. Cover and simmer until thickest pieces of chicken are done, about 45 minutes. Remove chicken from broth; strain broth. Refrigerate chicken and broth separately until cool.

Remove chicken from bones and skin. Finely chop enough dark meat to measure ¾ cup; cover and refrigerate. Cut remaining chicken into bite-size pieces; add to broth. Cover and refrigerate. Prepare Tortellini.

Skim fat from broth. Heat broth and 2 cups water to boiling. Add Tortellini. Heat to boiling; reduce heat. Cover and simmer until Tortellini are tender, about 30 minutes. Sprinkle each serving with snipped parsley and serve with cheese.

TORTELLINI

1½ cups all-purpose flour
1 egg
1 egg, separated
2 tablespoons water
1 tablespoon olive or vegetable oil
1 teaspoon salt
2 tablespoons grated Parmesan cheese
⅛ teaspoon grated lemon peel
⅛ teaspoon salt
Dash of ground mace
Dash of pepper

Make a well in center of flour; add 1 egg, 1 egg white, the water, oil and 1 teaspoon salt. Stir with fork until mixed; gather dough into a ball. (Sprinkle with a few drops water if dry.) Knead dough on lightly floured board until smooth and elastic, about 5 minutes. Cover and let rest 10 minutes.

Mix reserved ¾ cup chicken, the egg yolk, cheese, lemon peel, ⅛ teaspoon salt, the mace and pepper. Divide dough into halves. Roll one half on lightly floured board into 12-inch square. Cut into twenty 2-inch circles. Place ¼ teaspoon filling on center of each circle.

Moisten edge of each circle with water. Fold circle in half; press edge with fork to seal. Shape into rings by stretching tips of each half circle slightly; wrap ring around index finger. Moisten one tip with water; gently press tips together. Repeat with remaining dough. Place on tray; cover and refrigerate no longer than 24 hours.

Do-Ahead Tip: Freeze broth and Tortellini separately no longer than 2 weeks. To serve, heat broth and 2 cups water to boiling; continue as directed except simmer 40 minutes.

Oriental-style Chicken Noodle Soup

4 SERVINGS

3 cups water
1 package (3 ounces) chicken flavor
  Oriental-style 3-minute noodles
2 cups cut-up cooked chicken
2 medium stalks bok choy (with leaves),
  cut into ¼-inch slices
1 medium carrot, sliced

Heat water to boiling in 3-quart saucepan. Break apart block of noodles into water; stir in chicken, bok choy and carrot.

Heat to boiling; reduce heat. Simmer uncovered 3 minutes, stirring occasionally. Stir in flavor packet from noodle package and sesame oil, if desired.

Following pages: Chicken Soup with Tortellini

Hearty Vegetable Soup

*1 cup chopped fully cooked smoked ham
(about 4 ounces)*
1 medium onion, sliced
2 cloves garlic, crushed
2 tablespoons olive or vegetable oil
3 cups water
*1 tablespoon snipped fresh oregano leaves
or 1 teaspoon dried oregano leaves*
*1½ teaspoons snipped fresh thyme leaves
or ½ teaspoon dried thyme leaves*
¼ teaspoon pepper
*1 can (16 ounces) whole tomatoes,
undrained*
1 cup uncooked spiral or elbow macaroni
2 medium potatoes, cut into ½-inch pieces
*1 can (20 ounces) cannellini beans or
1 can (15 ounces) red kidney beans,
drained*
1 small zucchini, thinly sliced
⅓ cup grated Parmesan cheese

Cook and stir ham, onion and garlic in oil in Dutch oven over medium heat until onion is tender, about 5 minutes. Stir in water, oregano, thyme, pepper and tomatoes; break up the tomatoes. Heat to boiling. Stir in macaroni and potatoes; reduce heat. Cook uncovered until macaroni is tender, about 10 minutes.

Stir in beans and zucchini. Cook just until zucchini is crisp-tender, about 3 minutes. Sprinkle with cheese.

Italian Vegetable Soup

1 cup water
½ cup dried great northern, navy or kidney beans
4 cups chicken broth
2 small tomatoes, chopped
2 medium carrots, sliced
1 stalk celery, sliced
1 medium onion, chopped
1 clove garlic, chopped
½ cup uncooked macaroni (shells, bows or elbow macaroni)
1 tablespoon snipped parsley
1 teaspoon salt
1½ teaspoons snipped fresh basil leaves or ½ teaspoon dried basil leaves
⅛ teaspoon pepper
1 bay leaf
4 ounces green beans, cut into 1-inch pieces (about ¾ cup)
2 small zucchini, cut into 1-inch slices
Grated Parmesan cheese

Heat water and dried beans to boiling in Dutch oven; boil 2 minutes. Remove from heat. Cover and let stand 1 hour. Add enough water to cover beans if necessary. Heat to boiling; reduce heat. Cover and simmer until tender, 1 to 1½ hours (do not boil or beans will burst).

Add chicken broth, tomatoes, carrots, celery, onion, garlic, macaroni, parsley, salt, basil, pepper and bay leaf to beans. Heat to boiling; reduce heat. Cover and simmer 15 minutes. Add green beans and zucchini. Heat to boiling; reduce heat. Cover and simmer until macaroni and vegetables are tender, 10 to 15 minutes. Remove bay leaf. Serve with cheese.

Minestrone with Pesto

4 cups raw vegetable pieces*
2 ounces uncooked spaghetti, broken into 2- to 3-inch pieces, or 1/2 cup uncooked macaroni
1 1/2 teaspoons snipped fresh basil leaves or 1/2 teaspoon dried basil leaves
1/8 teaspoon pepper
1 medium onion, chopped
1 clove garlic, finely chopped
1 can (15 ounces) kidney or garbanzo beans, undrained
2 cans (10 1/2 ounces each) condensed beef broth
2 broth cans water
5 ounces spinach, cut crosswise into 1/4-inch strips
Pesto Sauce (page 89) or commercially prepared pesto

Heat all ingredients except spinach and Pesto Sauce to boiling in 4-quart Dutch oven; reduce heat.

Cover and simmer until vegetables and spaghetti are tender, about 10 minutes. Stir in spinach until wilted. Serve with Pesto Sauce and, if desired, grated Parmesan cheese.

*Sliced carrots, celery, zucchini or yellow summer squash, green or yellow beans, cut into 1-inch slices, chopped tomatoes or shelled peas can be used.

Meatball Minestrone

Mini Meatballs (below)
1 can (28 ounces) whole tomatoes,
    undrained
1 can (15 ounces) kidney beans,
    undrained
1 can (12 ounces) vacuum-packed whole
    kernel corn, undrained
2 cups water
½ cup dry red wine or water
1 tablespoon Italian seasoning
1 teaspoon salt
½ teaspoon pepper
2 stalks celery, sliced (about 1 cup)
1 medium onion, chopped (about ½ cup)
1 cup elbow spaghetti or broken spaghetti
2 zucchini, sliced (about 2 cups)

Prepare Mini Meatballs. Mix tomatoes, beans, corn, water, wine, Italian seasoning, salt, pepper, celery and onion in 4-quart Dutch oven; break up tomatoes with fork. Add meatballs, spaghetti and zucchini. Heat to boiling; reduce heat. Cover and simmer, stirring occasionally, until spaghetti and zucchini are tender, about 12 minutes. Serve with grated Parmesan cheese, if desired.

MINI MEATBALLS

1 pound ground beef
1 egg
1 small onion, chopped (about ¼ cup)
¼ cup dry bread crumbs
¼ cup milk
1 clove garlic, crushed
2 tablespoons snipped fresh parsley
1 teaspoon fennel seed
1½ teaspoons snipped fresh basil leaves
    or ½ teaspoon dried basil leaves
½ teaspoon salt
⅛ teaspoon pepper

Mix all ingredients. Shape mixture into about thirty-six 1-inch balls. (For ease in shaping meatballs, occasionally wet hands with cold water.) Place meatballs in lightly greased jelly roll pan, 15½ × 10½ × 1 inch, or 2 rectangular pans, 13 × 9 × 2 inches. Bake uncovered in 400° oven until brown, 15 to 20 minutes; cool slightly.

Following pages: Minestrone with Pesto

Chunky Beef Noodle Soup

4 SERVINGS

1 pound beef boneless round steak, cut
    into ¾-inch pieces
1 large onion, chopped
2 cloves garlic, finely chopped
1 tablespoon vegetable oil
2 cups water
2 teaspoons chili powder
1½ teaspoons salt
½ teaspoon dried oregano leaves
1 can (16 ounces) whole tomatoes,
    undrained
1 can (10½ ounces) condensed beef broth
2 ounces uncooked egg noodles (about
    1 cup)
1 medium green pepper, coarsely chopped
¼ cup snipped fresh parsley

Cook and stir beef steak, onion and garlic in
oil in 4-quart Dutch oven until beef is brown,
about 15 minutes. Stir in water, chili powder,
salt, oregano, tomatoes and broth; break up
tomatoes. Heat to boiling; reduce heat. Cover
and simmer until beef is tender, 1½ to 2 hours.

Skim excess fat from soup. Stir noodles and
green pepper into soup. Heat to boiling; reduce heat. Simmer uncovered until noodles
are tender, about 10 minutes. Stir in parsley.

Tortellini and Sausage Soup

6 SERVINGS

1 pound bulk Italian sausage
1 medium onion, coarsely chopped
3 cups water
1½ teaspoons snipped fresh basil leaves
    or ½ teaspoon dried basil leaves
1½ teaspoons snipped fresh oregano
    leaves or ½ teaspoon dried oregano
    leaves
2 carrots, sliced
1 medium zucchini or yellow summer
    squash, halved and sliced
2 cans (10¾ ounces) condensed tomato
    soup
8 ounces uncooked dried or frozen cheese-
    or meat-filled tortellini (2 cups)
Grated Parmesan cheese

Cook and stir sausage and onion in 4-quart
Dutch oven until sausage is light brown; drain.
Stir in remaining ingredients except cheese.

Heat to boiling; reduce heat. Cover and simmer until vegetables and tortellini are tender,
about 20 minutes. Serve with cheese.

PASTA AND CHEESE

Fettuccine with Four Cheeses

4 SERVINGS

¼ cup margarine or butter
½ cup half-and-half
½ cup shredded Gruyère cheese
  (2 ounces)
¼ cup grated Parmesan cheese
½ teaspoon salt
⅛ teaspoon freshly ground pepper
1 clove garlic, finely chopped
8 ounces uncooked fettuccine or Green
  Fettuccine (page 82)
2 tablespoons olive oil
½ cup crumbled Gorgonzola cheese
½ cup shredded mozzarella cheese
  (2 ounces)
1 tablespoon snipped fresh parsley

Heat margarine and half-and-half in 2-quart saucepan over low heat until margarine is melted. Stir in Gruyère cheese, Parmesan cheese, salt, pepper and garlic. Cook, stirring occasionally, 5 minutes.

Cook fettuccine as directed on package except add oil to boiling water; drain. Add hot fettuccine to sauce; add Gorgonzola cheese and mozzarella cheese. Toss with 2 forks; sprinkle with parsley.

Following pages: Fettuccine with Four Cheeses

Spaghetti alla Carbonara

6 SERVINGS

6 slices bacon, cut into ½-inch squares
16 ounces thin spaghetti
3 eggs, beaten
1 cup grated Parmesan cheese
Freshly ground pepper

Fry bacon over medium heat until almost crisp. Cook spaghetti as directed on package. Drain; do not rinse. Return to pot. Immediately add bacon, bacon fat, eggs and ½ cup of the cheese to spaghetti; toss over low heat until egg coats spaghetti and appears cooked. Serve with remaining cheese; sprinkle with pepper.

Fettuccine with Cheese and Cream

6 SERVINGS

8 ounces uncooked fettuccine
½ cup margarine or butter
½ cup whipping cream
¾ cup grated Parmesan cheese
½ teaspoon salt
Dash of pepper
2 teaspoons snipped fresh parsley

Cook fettuccine as directed on package; drain. Heat margarine and whipping cream over low heat until margarine is melted. Stir in cheese, salt and pepper. Pour sauce over hot noodles, stirring until noodles are well coated. Sprinkle with parsley.

Noodles Romanoff

8 SERVINGS

8 ounces uncooked wide egg noodles
2 cups dairy sour cream
¼ cup grated Parmesan cheese
1 tablespoon snipped fresh chives
1 teaspoon salt
⅛ teaspoon pepper
1 large clove garlic, crushed
2 tablespoons margarine or butter
¼ cup grated Parmesan cheese

Cook noodles as directed on package; drain. Mix sour cream, ¼ cup cheese, the chives, salt, pepper and garlic. Stir margarine into hot noodles; stir in sour cream mixture. Arrange on warm serving platter; sprinkle with ¼ cup cheese.

Rotini with Havarti and Herbs

6 SERVINGS

8 ounces uncooked vegetable-flavored
   rotini (about 3 cups)
2 teaspoons snipped fresh savory leaves
   or 1/2 teaspoon dried savory leaves,
   crushed
1/4 cup whipping cream
6 ounces herb-flavored Havarti cheese,
   shredded
2 small summer squash, thinly sliced
Coarsely ground pepper

Cook rotini as directed on package except add savory to water; drain. Return rotini to pot.

Stir in whipping cream, cheese and squash until cheese is melted. Arrange on platter; sprinkle with pepper. Garnish with fresh savory leaves, if desired.

Macaroni con Queso

4 SERVINGS

Chile con Queso (below)
4 ounces uncooked elbow macaroni or
   macaroni shells (about 1 cup)
1 large tomato, chopped (about 1 cup)
1 tablespoon snipped fresh cilantro
1 cup shredded Cheddar or Monterey
   Jack cheese (4 ounces)
1/4 cup crushed tortilla chips

CHILE CON QUESO

1 cup shredded Cheddar or Monterey
   Jack cheese (4 ounces)
1 can (4 ounces) chopped green chilies,
   drained
1/2 cup milk
1/4 cup half-and-half
2 tablespoons finely chopped onion
2 teaspoons ground cumin
1/2 teaspoon salt

Heat oven to 375°. Prepare Chile con Queso. Cook macaroni as directed on package; drain.

Mix macaroni, Chile con Queso, tomato and cilantro in ungreased 1 1/2-quart casserole. Sprinkle with cheese and tortilla chips. Bake uncovered until hot, about 30 minutes.

Heat all ingredients over low heat, stirring constantly, until cheese is melted.

Following pages: Macaroni con Queso

Macaroni and Cheese

1 to 1½ cups uncooked elbow macaroni, rigatoni or spinach egg noodles
(about 6 ounces)
¼ cup margarine or butter
1 small onion, chopped (about ¼ cup)
½ teaspoon salt
¼ teaspoon pepper
¼ cup all-purpose flour
1¾ cups milk
8 ounces process sharp American or Swiss
cheese, cut into ½-inch cubes

Cook macaroni as directed on package; drain. Cook and stir margarine, onion, salt and pepper over medium heat until onion is tender. Stir in flour. Cook over low heat, stirring constantly, until mixture is smooth and bubbly; remove from heat. Stir in milk. Heat to boiling, stirring constantly. Boil and stir 1 minute; remove from heat. Stir in cheese until melted.

Place macaroni in ungreased 1½-quart casserole. Stir cheese sauce into macaroni. Bake uncovered in 375° oven 30 minutes.

HAM MACARONI AND CHEESE: Stir 1 cup cut-up fully cooked smoked ham into cheese sauce.

OLIVE MACARONI AND CHEESE: Stir ¼ cup chopped pimiento-stuffed green olives into cheese sauce.

PEPPER MACARONI AND CHEESE: Stir ⅓ cup chopped green and/or red peppers or 1 can (4 ounces) green chilies, drained and chopped, into cheese sauce.

TUNA MACARONI AND CHEESE: Stir 1 can (6½ ounces) tuna, drained, into cheese sauce.

Macaroni and Cheese with Tomato

4 SERVINGS

4 slices bacon, cut into 1-inch pieces
1 medium onion, chopped
1 medium green pepper, chopped
1 package (7 ounces) uncooked elbow
   macaroni (2 cups)
1 can (10¾ ounces) condensed tomato
   soup
1½ soup cans water
2 cups shredded American or colby cheese
   (8 ounces)

Cook bacon in 10-inch skillet, stirring frequently, until crisp. Stir in onion and green pepper; cook and stir until vegetables are tender. Stir in macaroni, soup and water.

Heat to boiling, stirring once or twice; reduce heat. Cover and simmer, stirring occasionally, until macaroni is tender, about 20 minutes. Stir in cheese until melted. Top each serving with buttered bread or cracker crumbs, if desired.

Double Cheese Tortellini

4 SERVINGS

2 cans (16 ounces each) stewed tomatoes
1½ teaspoons snipped fresh oregano
   leaves or ½ teaspoon dried oregano
   leaves
1 package (7 ounces) uncooked dried
   cheese-filled tortellini
1 cup shredded Cheddar cheese (4 ounces)

Heat tomatoes and oregano to boiling in 3-quart saucepan; stir in tortellini. Heat to boiling; reduce heat.

Boil gently, stirring occasionally, until tortellini are of desired doneness, 20 to 25 minutes. (Add 1 to 2 tablespoons water during last 5 minutes of cooking, if necessary, to prevent sticking.) Top each serving with ¼ cup cheese.

Cheese Lasagne

Egg Noodles (page 79) or 12 uncooked
  lasagne noodles
½ cup margarine or butter
½ cup all-purpose flour
½ teaspoon salt
4 cups milk
1 cup shredded Swiss cheese
1 cup shredded mozzarella cheese
½ cup grated Parmesan cheese
2 cups creamed cottage cheese
¼ cup snipped fresh parsley
1 tablespoon snipped fresh basil leaves
  or 1 teaspoon dried basil leaves
½ teaspoon salt
1½ teaspoons snipped fresh oregano
  leaves or ½ teaspoon dried oregano
  leaves
2 cloves garlic, crushed
½ cup grated Parmesan cheese

Prepare Egg Noodles as directed except divide dough into halves. Roll one half into rectangle, 13 × 12 inches; cut rectangle lengthwise into 6 strips, 13 × 2 inches. Repeat with other half. Spread strips on wire rack; let stand until dry, at least 1 hour.

Heat margarine in 2-quart saucepan over low heat until melted. Blend in flour and ½ teaspoon salt. Cook over low heat, stirring constantly, until smooth and bubbly; remove from heat. Stir in milk. Heat to boiling, stirring constantly. Boil and stir 1 minute. Stir in Swiss cheese, mozzarella cheese and ½ cup Parmesan cheese. Stir over low heat until cheeses are melted. Mix cottage cheese, parsley, basil, ½ teaspoon salt, the oregano and garlic.

Spread ¼ of the cheese sauce mixture in ungreased rectangular baking dish, 13 × 9 × 2 inches; top with 4 uncooked noodles. Spread 1 cup of the cottage cheese mixture over noodles; spread with ¼ of the cheese sauce mixture. Repeat with 4 noodles, the remaining cottage cheese mixture, ¼ of the cheese sauce mixture, the remaining noodles and the remaining cheese sauce mixture. Sprinkle with ½ cup Parmesan cheese. Cook uncovered in 350° oven until noodles are done, 35 to 40 minutes. Let stand 10 minutes before cutting.

· 3 ·

PASTA AND VEGETABLES

Spaghetti with Mushrooms

6 SERVINGS

7 ounces uncooked spaghetti
5 ounces mushrooms, sliced (2 cups)
2 tablespoons margarine or butter
2 tablespoons all-purpose flour
2 tablespoons lemon juice
1/2 teaspoon salt
1/4 teaspoon pepper
2 cups milk
3 tablespoons snipped fresh parsley

Cook spaghetti as directed on package; drain. Cook and stir mushrooms in margarine in 3-quart saucepan over medium heat until tender. Stir in flour, lemon juice, salt and pepper. Cook over low heat, stirring constantly, until mixture is smooth and bubbly; remove from heat.

Gradually stir in milk. Heat to boiling, stirring constantly. Boil and stir 1 minute. Stir in hot spaghetti and parsley. Cover and let stand 10 minutes.

Spaghetti with Artichoke Hearts

6 SERVINGS

8 ounces uncooked thin spaghetti
1 can (14 ounces) artichoke hearts
2 medium tomatoes, chopped (about 2 cups)
3 green onions, chopped
1 1/2 teaspoons snipped fresh oregano leaves or 1/2 teaspoon dried oregano leaves
1/4 teaspoon salt

Cook spaghetti in 3 quarts boiling salted water (1 tablespoon salt) until tender, 4 to 6 minutes; drain. Drain artichoke hearts, reserving 1/4 cup liquid. Cut artichokes into halves. Cook and stir artichokes, tomatoes, onions, oregano, salt and reserved artichoke liquid just until hot, about 7 minutes; toss with hot spaghetti.

29

Broccoli-Mushroom Spaghetti

5 SERVINGS

*1 package (10 ounces) frozen chopped
    broccoli*
*1 jar (4¹/₂ ounces) sliced mushrooms,
    drained*
¹/₄ cup margarine or butter
¹/₂ teaspoon salt
¹/₈ teaspoon pepper
1 package (7 ounces) spaghetti
¹/₂ cup grated Parmesan cheese
1 tablespoon lemon juice

Cook broccoli as directed on package; drain. Return broccoli to pot. Stir in mushrooms, margarine, salt and pepper. Heat over low heat, stirring occasionally, until mushrooms are hot, about 5 minutes. Cook spaghetti as directed on package; drain. Toss spaghetti, broccoli mixture, Parmesan cheese and lemon juice. Serve with additional grated Parmesan cheese, if desired.

Vermicelli and Spinach

8 SERVINGS

8 ounces uncooked vermicelli
*6 slices red onion (¹/₄ inch thick), sepa-
    rated into rings*
2 cloves garlic, crushed
2 tablespoons olive or vegetable oil
*12 ounces spinach, cut crosswise into
    ¹/₂-inch strips (about 12 cups)*
2 tablespoons lemon juice
*1 tablespoon snipped fresh tarragon
    leaves or 1 teaspoon dried tarragon
    leaves*
¹/₄ teaspoon salt
Freshly ground pepper
*¹/₄ cup crumbled Gorgonzola or blue
    cheese*

Cook vermicelli as directed on package; drain. Cook and stir onion and garlic in oil in 12-inch skillet over medium heat until onion is almost tender, about 5 minutes. Stir in spinach, lemon juice, tarragon, salt and pepper. Cook and stir until spinach is slightly limp, about 2 minutes. Toss with hot vermicelli; sprinkle with cheese.

Vermicelli with Lemony Green Vegetables

4 SERVINGS

1 package (7 ounces) uncooked vermicelli
4 cups mixed bite-size pieces green vegetables (asparagus, broccoli, Chinese pea pods, green beans, zucchini)
1/4 cup margarine or butter
1 tablespoon grated lemon peel
1/2 cup milk
1 package (3 ounces) cream cheese, cut into cubes and softened
1/2 cup grated Parmesan cheese
Salt and pepper to taste

Cook vermicelli as directed on package; drain. Cook vegetables in margarine in 10-inch skillet over medium heat, stirring frequently, until crisp-tender, about 7 minutes; toss with lemon peel. Remove vegetables; keep warm.

Heat milk and cream cheese in skillet until smooth and creamy; stir in Parmesan cheese, salt and pepper. Toss with hot vermicelli. Serve vegetables over vermicelli and, if desired, with lemon wedges and coarsely ground pepper.

Mostaccioli with Bell Pepper and Basil

4 SERVINGS

1 green pepper, cut into 1/4-inch strips
1 onion, sliced and separated into rings
1 clove garlic, crushed
2 tablespoons olive or vegetable oil
1 1/2 cups uncooked mostaccioli
1 medium tomato, coarsely chopped
1 tablespoon snipped fresh basil leaves or 1 teaspoon dried basil leaves
1/4 teaspoon salt
Freshly ground pepper
2 tablespoons grated Romano cheese

Cook and stir green pepper, onion and garlic in oil over medium heat until pepper is tender, about 10 minutes. Cook mostaccioli as directed on package; drain. Stir tomato, basil, salt and pepper into green pepper mixture; heat until hot. Toss with hot mostaccioli; sprinkle with grated cheese.

Following pages: Vermicelli with Lemony Green Vegetables

Macaroni with Marinated Tomatoes

6 SERVINGS

2 medium tomatoes, chopped (about
  2 cups)
2 green onions (with tops), chopped
2 cloves garlic, finely chopped
1/4 cup snipped fresh parsley
1/2 teaspoon salt
1 1/2 teaspoons snipped fresh basil leaves
  or 1/2 teaspoon dried basil leaves
1/8 teaspoon coarsely cracked pepper
2 tablespoons olive or vegetable oil
1 package (7 ounces) macaroni shells

Mix tomatoes, onions, garlic, parsley, salt, basil, pepper and oil. Cover and refrigerate at least 2 hours but no longer than 24 hours.

Prepare macaroni as directed on package; drain. Immediately toss with tomato mixture.

Macaroni and Vegetables

6 SERVINGS

1 cup uncooked spiral or elbow macaroni (about 4 ounces)
1 medium zucchini, cut into 3/8-inch slices
1 medium tomato, coarsely chopped
  (about 1 cup)
1 medium onion, chopped (about 1/2 cup)
1 small green pepper, chopped (about
  1/2 cup)
1 large clove garlic, finely chopped
2 tablespoons olive or vegetable oil
1 teaspoon salt
3/4 teaspoon snipped fresh basil leaves or
  1/4 teaspoon dried basil leaves
1/8 teaspoon pepper

Cook macaroni as directed on package; drain. Cook and stir zucchini, tomato, onion, green pepper and garlic in oil in 10-inch skillet over medium heat 3 minutes. Stir in macaroni and the remaining ingredients. Cook, stirring occasionally, until zucchini is crisp-tender, about 3 minutes. Serve with grated Parmesan cheese, if desired.

Rigatoni and Tomatoes

3 medium tomatoes, chopped (about
   3 cups)
3 tablespoons olive or vegetable oil
2 tablespoons snipped fresh basil leaves
   or 2 teaspoons dried basil leaves
2 tablespoons capers
1 tablespoon lemon juice
1 teaspoon sugar
1/2 teaspoon salt
1/8 teaspoon crushed red pepper
1 clove garlic, finely chopped
3 cups uncooked rigatoni
1/4 cup grated Parmesan or Romano
   cheese

Mix all ingredients except rigatoni and cheese. Cover and refrigerate at least 2 hours but no longer than 24 hours.

Prepare rigatoni as directed on package; drain. Immediately toss with tomato mixture. Serve immediately, or cover and refrigerate until chilled. Sprinkle with cheese.

Zucchini Lasagne

3 cups chunky-style spaghetti sauce
1 medium zucchini, shredded
6 uncooked lasagne noodles
1 cup ricotta or small curd creamed cottage cheese
1/4 cup grated Parmesan cheese
1 tablespoon snipped fresh oregano leaves
   or 1 teaspoon dried oregano leaves
2 cups shredded mozzarella cheese
   (8 ounces)

Mix spaghetti sauce and zucchini. Spread 1 cup mixture in ungreased rectangular baking dish, 11 × 7 × 1½ inches; top with 3 uncooked noodles. Mix ricotta cheese, Parmesan cheese and oregano; spread over noodles in dish. Spread with 1 cup of the sauce mixture.

Top with remaining noodles, sauce mixture and the mozzarella cheese. Bake uncovered in 350° oven until hot and bubbly, about 45 minutes. Let stand 15 minutes before cutting.

Following pages: Rigatoni and Tomatoes

Vegetable Lasagne

White Sauce (below)
1 package (10 ounces) frozen chopped
 spinach
2 cups creamed cottage cheese
½ cup grated Parmesan cheese
1 tablespoon snipped fresh basil leaves
 or 1 teaspoon dried basil leaves
1½ teaspoons snipped fresh oregano
 leaves or ½ teaspoon dried oregano
 leaves
¼ teaspoon pepper
12 lasagne noodles, cooked and drained
1½ cups shredded mozzarella cheese
1 can (8 ounces) mushroom stems and
 pieces, drained and coarsely chopped
2 medium carrots, coarsely shredded
1 medium onion, chopped (about ½ cup)
1 medium green pepper, chopped (about
 1 cup)

Prepare White Sauce. Rinse frozen spinach under running cold water to separate. Drain; pat dry with paper towels. Mix spinach, cottage cheese, ¼ cup of the Parmesan cheese, the basil, oregano and pepper. Arrange 4 noodles in ungreased 13 × 9 × 2-inch baking dish. Top with half of the cheese mixture, ½ cup of the mozzarella cheese and 4 noodles. Layer mushrooms, carrots, onion and green pepper on noodles. Spread half of the White Sauce over top; sprinkle with ½ cup of the mozzarella cheese. Top with remaining noodles, cheese mixture, White Sauce and mozzarella cheese; sprinkle with remaining ¼ cup Parmesan cheese.

Cook uncovered in 350° oven until hot and bubbly, about 35 minutes. Let stand 10 minutes before cutting.

WHITE SAUCE

⅓ cup margarine or butter
⅓ cup all-purpose flour
1 teaspoon salt
⅛ teaspoon ground nutmeg
3 cups milk

Heat margarine in 1-quart saucepan over low heat until melted. Stir in flour, salt and nutmeg. Cook over low heat, stirring constantly, until bubbly; remove from heat. Stir in milk. Heat to boiling, stirring constantly. Boil and stir 1 minute; cover and keep warm. (If sauce thickens, beat in small amount milk.)

PASTA AND SEAFOOD

Scallops in Cream Sauce

6 SERVINGS

1 pound scallops
1 green onion (with top), thinly sliced
¼ cup margarine or butter
¼ teaspoon salt
¼ cup dry white wine
2 teaspoons cornstarch
½ cup whipping cream
4 cups hot cooked spinach noodles or
*   fettuccine*
½ cup finely shredded Swiss cheese

If scallops are large, cut into halves. Cook and stir onion in margarine in 10-inch skillet over medium-high heat until tender. Stir in scallops and salt. Cook, stirring frequently, until scallops are white, 3 to 4 minutes.

Mix wine and cornstarch; stir into scallop mixture. Heat to boiling, stirring constantly. Boil and stir 1 minute; reduce heat to medium. Stir in whipping cream. Heat until hot, 1 to 2 minutes. Toss noodles and cheese. Spoon scallop mixture over noodles. Serve with freshly ground pepper if desired.

Southwest Sautéed Scallops

6 SERVINGS

2 cups water
1 dried red chili
¼ cup sliced green onions (with tops)
2 tablespoons margarine or butter
2 tablespoons lime juice
2 pounds sea scallops
2 cups cubed fresh pineapple
*1 cup Chinese pea pod halves (about
    3 ounces)*
3 cups hot cooked fettuccine

Heat water to boiling in 1-quart saucepan. Add chili. Boil 5 minutes; drain. Remove stem and seeds; finely chop chili.

Cook and stir onions, margarine, lime juice and chili in 10-inch skillet until margarine is melted. Carefully stir in scallops. Cook over medium heat, stirring frequently, until scallops are white, about 12 minutes.

Stir in pineapple and pea pods; heat until hot. Remove scallop mixture with slotted spoon; keep warm.

Heat liquid in skillet to boiling. Boil until slightly thickened and reduced to about half. Spoon scallop mixture onto fettuccine; pour liquid over scallop mixture.

Salmon with Artichokes

8 SERVINGS

4 slices bacon, cut into ½-inch pieces
1 medium onion, sliced
1 medium stalk celery, diagonally sliced
*1 package (9 ounces) frozen artichoke
    hearts*
1 package (10 ounces) frozen green peas
¼ cup water
½ teaspoon salt
*¾ teaspoon snipped fresh tarragon leaves
    or ¼ teaspoon dried tarragon leaves*
¼ teaspoon pepper
*1 can (14¾ ounces) salmon, drained and
    flaked*
1 jar (2 ounces) diced pimiento, drained
1 tablespoon lemon juice
3 cups hot cooked spaghetti

Fry bacon in 10-inch skillet until crisp. Remove with slotted spoon and drain; reserve. Cook and stir onion and celery in bacon fat until onion is tender, about 5 minutes. Stir in artichokes, peas, water, salt, tarragon and pepper. Heat to boiling; reduce heat. Cover and simmer until vegetables are tender, about 10 minutes. Stir in salmon, pimiento and lemon juice; heat just until salmon is hot. Toss with spaghetti; sprinkle with reserved bacon.

TUNA WITH ARTICHOKES: Substitute 2 cans (6½ ounces each) tuna in water, drained, for the canned salmon.

Spaghetti with Tomato-and-Anchovy Sauce

6 SERVINGS

1 medium onion, chopped
1 clove garlic, chopped
2 tablespoons olive or vegetable oil
1 can (8 ounces) tomato sauce
1 can (1¾ ounces) anchovies, drained
    and chopped
¼ cup snipped fresh parsley
1½ teaspoons snipped fresh oregano
    leaves or ½ teaspoon dried oregano
    leaves
¼ teaspoon salt
⅛ teaspoon pepper
¼ cup dry bread crumbs
1 tablespoon olive oil, margarine or
    butter
8 ounces uncooked spaghetti

Cook and stir onion and garlic in 2 tablespoons oil in 10-inch skillet until onion is tender. Stir in tomato sauce, anchovies, parsley, oregano, salt and pepper. Heat to boiling; reduce heat. Cover and simmer 15 minutes.

Cook and stir bread crumbs in 1 tablespoon oil until golden brown. Cook spaghetti as directed on package; drain. Toss spaghetti with sauce; sprinkle with bread crumbs.

Creamy Tuna Casserole

6 SERVINGS

8 ounces uncooked noodles
1 can (12½ ounces) tuna, drained
1 can (4 ounces) sliced mushrooms,
    drained
1 jar (2 ounces) sliced pimientos, drained
1½ cups dairy sour cream
¾ cup milk
1 teaspoon salt
¼ teaspoon pepper
¼ cup dry bread crumbs
¼ cup grated Parmesan cheese
2 tablespoons margarine or butter, melted
Snipped fresh parsley

Cook noodles as directed on package; drain. Mix noodles, tuna, mushrooms, pimientos, sour cream, milk, salt and pepper in 2-quart casserole. Mix bread crumbs, cheese and margarine; sprinkle over tuna mixture.

Bake uncovered in 350° oven until hot and bubbly, 35 to 40 minutes. Sprinkle with parsley.

Follwing pages: Southwest Sautéed Scallops, left, and Shrimp Lo Mein, right (page 44)

Shrimp Lo Mein

¾ pound fresh or frozen raw shrimp
1 teaspoon cornstarch
½ teaspoon sesame oil
¼ teaspoon salt
⅛ teaspoon white pepper
8 ounces bok choy (about 4 large stalks)
6 ounces pea pods
4 ounces mushrooms
2 green onions (with tops)
3 tablespoons cornstarch
3 tablespoons cold water
2 quarts water
1 package (8 ounces) Chinese egg noodles
2 tablespoons vegetable oil
1 teaspoon chopped gingerroot
1 teaspoon finely chopped garlic
2 tablespoons vegetable oil
¼ cup oyster sauce
1 teaspoon salt
1 cup chicken broth

Peel shrimp. (If shrimp are frozen, do not thaw; peel under running cold water.) Make shallow cut lengthwise down back of each shrimp; wash out sand vein. Cut shrimp lengthwise into halves. Toss shrimp, 1 teaspoon cornstarch, the sesame oil, ¼ teaspoon salt and the white pepper in glass or plastic bowl. Cover and refrigerate 20 minutes.

Separate bok choy leaves from stems. Cut leaves into 2-inch pieces; cut stems diagonally into ¼-inch slices (do not combine leaves and stems). Remove strings from pea pods. Place pea pods in boiling water. Cover and boil 1 minute; drain. Immediately rinse under running cold water; drain. Cut mushrooms into ½-inch slices. Cut green onions into 2-inch pieces. Mix 3 tablespoons cornstarch and 3 tablespoons water.

Heat 2 quarts water to boiling in Dutch oven. Stir in noodles. Cook uncovered over medium heat until noodles are soft and can be separated, about 5 minutes; drain. Keep noodles warm in 300° oven.

Heat wok or 12-inch skillet until 1 or 2 drops of water bubble and skitter when sprinkled in wok. Add 2 tablespoons vegetable oil; rotate wok to coat side. Add shrimp, gingerroot and garlic; stir-fry until shrimp are pink. Remove shrimp from wok.

Add 2 tablespoons oil to wok; rotate to coat side. Add bok choy stems; stir-fry 1 minute. Add bok choy leaves, mushrooms, oyster sauce and 1 teaspoon salt; stir-fry 1 minute. Stir in chicken broth; heat to boiling. Stir in cornstarch mixture; cook and stir until thickened, about 10 seconds. Add shrimp, pea pods and green onions; cook and stir 30 seconds. Serve over noodles.

Vermicelli with Smoked Fish and Gruyère 4 SERVINGS

8 ounces uncooked vermicelli
1 package (10 ounces) frozen chopped
  spinach
1 cup shredded Gruyère or Swiss cheese
  (4 ounces)
¼ cup half-and-half
2 tablespoons margarine or butter
½ pound smoked whitefish, skinned,
  boned and flaked into 1-inch pieces
  (about 2 cups)

Cook vermicelli as directed on package except add frozen spinach to water before heating water to boiling; drain.

Toss with cheese, half-and-half and margarine. Turn onto warm serving platter; arrange fish on top.

Tuna Spaghetti 5 SERVINGS

1 package (7 ounces) thin spaghetti
2 cloves garlic, finely chopped
¼ cup margarine or butter
¾ cup half-and-half
1 tablespoon snipped fresh basil leaves
  or 1 teaspoon dried basil leaves
¾ teaspoon snipped fresh oregano leaves
  or ¼ teaspoon dried oregano leaves
1 can (9¼ ounces) tuna, drained
½ cup sliced pimiento-stuffed olives
¼ cup grated Parmesan cheese

Cook spaghetti as directed on package; drain. Cook garlic in margarine in 2-quart saucepan until golden brown. Stir in half-and-half, basil and oregano. Heat to boiling. Stir in tuna, olives and cheese; boil and stir 1 minute. Pour over hot spaghetti. Sprinkle with snipped parsley, if desired.

Seafood Lasagne

1/2 cup margarine or butter
2 cloves garlic, crushed
1/2 cup all-purpose flour
1/2 teaspoon salt
2 cups milk
2 cups chicken broth
2 cups shredded mozzarella cheese
   (8 ounces)
1/2 cup sliced green onions (with tops)
1 tablespoon snipped fresh basil leaves or
   1 teaspoon dried basil leaves
1/4 teaspoon pepper
8 ounces uncooked lasagne noodles (9 or
   10 noodles)
1 cup creamed cottage cheese
1 can (7 1/2 ounces) crabmeat, drained and
   cartilage removed
1 can (4 1/2 ounces) tiny shrimp, drained
1/2 cup grated Parmesan cheese

Heat margarine in 3-quart saucepan over low heat until melted; add garlic. Stir in flour and salt. Cook, stirring constantly, until bubbly; remove from heat. Stir in milk and broth. Heat to boiling, stirring constantly. Boil and stir 1 minute. Stir in mozzarella cheese, onions, basil and pepper. Cook over low heat, stirring constantly, until cheese is melted.

Spread 1/4 of the cheese sauce (about 1 1/2 cups) in ungreased rectangular baking dish, 13 × 9 × 2 inches; top with 3 or 4 uncooked noodles, overlapping if necessary. Spread cottage cheese over noodles in dish. Repeat with 1/4 of the cheese sauce and 3 or 4 noodles. Top with crabmeat, shrimp, 1/4 of the cheese sauce, the remaining noodles and cheese sauce. Sprinkle with Parmesan cheese. Bake uncovered in 350° oven until noodles are done, 35 to 40 minutes. Let stand 15 minutes before cutting.

Seafood-stuffed Shells

15 uncooked jumbo macaroni shells
2 cups creamed cottage cheese (small curd)
1/4 cup plus 2 tablespoons milk
1 tablespoon lemon juice
1 teaspoon salt
1/8 teaspoon pepper
1/2 cup parsley sprigs
1 1/2 teaspoons snipped fresh basil leaves or 1/2 teaspoon dried basil leaves
2 cloves garlic, crushed
2 medium stalks celery, sliced (about 1 cup)
1 medium zucchini, coarsely shredded
1 medium onion, chopped (about 1/2 cup)
6 seafood legs, cut into 1/2-inch pieces
2 cans (4 1/2 ounces each) large shrimp, rinsed and drained
Salad greens

Prepare macaroni shells as directed on package; drain. Refrigerate at least 1 hour.

Place cottage cheese, milk, lemon juice, salt and pepper in blender container. Cover and blend on high speed, stopping blender occasionally to scrape sides, until smooth, about 2 minutes. Remove 1/2 cup; reserve. Add parsley, basil and garlic to remaining mixture in blender container. Cover and blend on high speed until smooth, about 45 seconds; refrigerate.

Mix celery, zucchini, onion, seafood legs, shrimp and reserved 1/2 cup cottage cheese mixture. Spoon into macaroni shells. Refrigerate at least 1 hour.

Place stuffed shells on salad greens; serve parsley mixture with shells. (If parsley mixture is too thick, stir in additional milk until of desired consistency.)

Following pages: Seafood-stuffed Shells

· 5 ·

PASTA AND POULTRY

Linguine with Chicken and Artichokes

4 SERVINGS

6 ounces uncooked linguine or spaghetti
1 jar (6 ounces) marinated artichoke
    hearts
2 tablespoons olive or vegetable oil
1 medium onion, coarsely chopped
2 cups cut-up cooked chicken or turkey
1 cup frozen green peas
1/8 pound sliced fully cooked smoked ham,
    cut into 1/4-inch strips (1/2 cup)*
1 tablespoon snipped fresh oregano leaves
    or 1 teaspoon dried oregano leaves
1/4 teaspoon pepper
1 container (8 ounces) dairy sour cream

Cook linguine as directed on package; drain.

Drain liquid from artichoke hearts into 10-inch skillet; cut artichoke hearts into halves and reserve. Add oil to artichoke liquid. Cook and stir onion in oil mixture until tender.

Stir artichoke hearts, chicken, peas, ham, oregano and pepper into onion mixture; cook and stir until hot. Remove from heat; stir in sour cream. Toss hot linguine with sauce.

*6 slices bacon, crisply cooked and crumbled, can be substituted for the ham.

Chinese Noodles with Chicken and Vegetables

4 SERVINGS

*4 boneless skinless chicken breast halves
  (about 1½ pounds)*
2 tablespoons vegetable oil
1 tablespoon finely chopped gingerroot
3 cloves garlic, finely chopped
*1 package (14 ounces) frozen chopped
  vegetables for stir-fry or chop suey
  (about 5 cups)*
*1 can (4 ounces) mushroom stems and
  pieces, undrained*
1 tablespoon instant chicken bouillon
½ cup cold water
1 tablespoon cornstarch
1 tablespoon soy sauce
5 ounces uncooked Chinese noodles
1 teaspoon sesame oil

Cut chicken into ¼-inch slices. Heat vegetable oil in 12-inch skillet or wok until hot. Cook and stir chicken, gingerroot and garlic in oil over medium-high heat until chicken is white, 3 to 4 minutes.

Stir in vegetables, mushrooms and bouillon (dry); cook and stir until vegetables are crisp-tender, about 5 minutes. Mix cold water, cornstarch and soy sauce; stir into chicken mixture. Heat to boiling, stirring constantly. Boil and stir 1 minute.

Cook noodles as directed on package; drain. Toss with sesame oil. Add noodles to chicken mixture in skillet; toss until well coated. Serve with additional soy sauce, if desired.

Chicken and Noodles

6 SERVINGS

1 package (10 ounces) spinach noodles
1 cup milk
2 cans (6¾ ounces each) chunk chicken
*1 can (4 ounces) mushroom stems and
  pieces, drained*
1 small onion, finely chopped
¼ cup grated Romano cheese
2 tablespoons margarine or butter, melted
⅛ teaspoon pepper

Cook noodles as directed on package; drain. Toss with remaining ingredients. Pour into ungreased 2-quart casserole. Cover and cook in 350° oven until hot, about 30 minutes. Stir before serving. Serve with additional grated Romano cheese, if desired.

Pasta Shells with Chicken and Broccoli

6 SERVINGS

1 cup chopped fresh broccoli
⅓ cup chopped onion
2 cloves garlic, finely chopped
1 carrot, cut into very thin strips
3 tablespoons vegetable oil
2 cups cut-up cooked chicken or turkey
1 teaspoon salt
2 medium tomatoes, chopped
4 cups hot cooked shell or cartwheel macaroni
⅓ cup grated Parmesan cheese
2 tablespoons snipped fresh parsley

Cook and stir broccoli, onion, garlic and carrot in oil in 10-inch skillet over medium heat until broccoli is crisp-tender, about 10 minutes.

Stir in chicken, salt and tomatoes; heat just until chicken is hot, about 3 minutes. Spoon over macaroni. Sprinkle with cheese and parsley.

Chicken and Fettuccine with Dijon Sauce

4 SERVINGS

6 ounces uncooked spinach fettuccine
½ cup chopped onion
2 cloves garlic, crushed
2 tablespoons margarine or butter
1 cup milk
½ cup chardonnay or dry white wine
2 tablespoons snipped fresh parsley
2 tablespoons Dijon-style mustard
1 package (3 ounces) cream cheese with chives, cut into cubes
1½ cups cut-up cooked chicken or turkey

Cook fettuccine as directed on package; drain. Cook and stir onion and garlic in margarine over medium heat in 3-quart saucepan until onion is tender. Add remaining ingredients except chicken; stir until cream cheese is melted. Add chicken and hot fettuccine to cheese mixture; toss until evenly coated. Heat just until hot. Garnish with chives and freshly ground pepper, if desired.

Chicken Livers with Pasta

1 package (7 ounces) elbow spaghetti
1/2 pound chicken livers, cut into 1-inch
   pieces
1 can (4 ounces) mushroom stems and
   pieces, drained
1 tablespoon vegetable oil
2 tablespoons margarine or butter
1/4 cup whipping cream
2 tablespoons grated Parmesan cheese
1 jar (2 ounces) diced pimiento, drained

Cook spaghetti as directed on package; drain. Cook livers and mushrooms in oil, stirring occasionally, until livers are brown, about 8 minutes. Toss spaghetti with margarine, cream and cheese. Stir in livers and pimiento.

Turkey and Ham Tetrazzini

7 ounces uncooked spaghetti
1 can (10¾ ounces) condensed cream of
   mushroom soup
1 can (10¾ ounces) condensed cream of
   chicken soup
¾ cup milk
2 tablespoons dry white wine
2 cups cut-up cooked turkey or chicken
1/2 cup cut-up fully cooked smoked ham
1 small green pepper, chopped (about
   1/2 cup)
1/2 cup halved pitted ripe olives
1/2 cup grated Parmesan cheese
1/4 cup toasted slivered almonds

Cook spaghetti as directed on package; rinse under running cold water and drain. Mix mushroom soup, chicken soup, milk and wine in ungreased 2-quart casserole. Stir in turkey, ham, spaghetti, green pepper and olives; sprinkle with cheese.

Bake uncovered in 375° oven until hot and bubbly, about 35 minutes. Sprinkle with almonds.

Following pages: Turkey and Ham Tetrazzini

Chipotle Fettuccine with Smoked Turkey in Corn Sauce

6 SERVINGS

Chipotle Fettuccine (page 83)
1½ cups whole kernel corn
½ cup water
1 small onion, chopped (about ¼ cup)
2 tablespoons margarine or butter
2 tablespoons all-purpose flour
½ teaspoon salt
¼ teaspoon pepper
1 cup milk
½ cup half-and-half
2 cups cut-up smoked turkey breast (about 12 ounces)

Prepare Chipotle Fettuccine. Heat corn, water and onion to boiling; reduce heat. Cover and simmer 5 minutes. Pour corn mixture into food processor workbowl fitted with steel blade or into blender container; cover and process until almost smooth.

Heat margarine in 2-quart saucepan over low heat until melted. Stir in flour, salt and pepper. Cook over low heat, stirring constantly, until smooth and bubbly. Remove from heat; stir in corn mixture, milk, half-and-half and turkey. Heat to boiling, stirring constantly. Boil and stir 1 minute. Toss with hot cooked fettuccine.

·6·

PASTA AND MEAT

Greek Macaroni with Beef and Cheese

6 SERVINGS

*7 ounces uncooked ziti or elbow maca-
roni (about 2 cups)*
¾ pound ground beef
1 small onion, chopped
1 can (15 ounces) tomato sauce
1 teaspoon salt
*1½ cups grated Kasseri, Parmesan or Ro-
mano cheese (6 ounces)*
⅛ teaspoon ground cinnamon
1¼ cups milk
3 tablespoons margarine or butter
2 eggs, beaten
⅛ teaspoon ground nutmeg

Cook macaroni as directed on package; drain. Cook and stir beef and onion in 10-inch skillet until beef is light brown; drain. Stir in tomato sauce and salt. Spread half the macaroni in greased square baking dish, 8 × 8 × 2 inches; cover with beef mixture. Mix ½ cup of the cheese and the cinnamon; sprinkle over beef mixture. Cover with remaining macaroni.

Cook and stir milk and margarine in 2-quart saucepan until margarine is melted. Remove from heat. Stir at least half the milk mixture gradually into beaten eggs. Blend into milk mixture in saucepan; pour over macaroni. Sprinkle with remaining 1 cup cheese. Cook uncovered in 325° oven until brown and center is set, about 50 minutes. Sprinkle with nutmeg. Garnish with parsley, if desired.

Stir-fried Noodles and Steak

4 medium dried black mushrooms
1 pound beef boneless sirloin or round
    steak
1 tablespoon vegetable oil
1 teaspoon cornstarch
1/2 teaspoon soy sauce
Dash of white pepper
1 package (about 6 ounces) rice stick
    noodles
12 ounces bean sprouts
4 ounces pea pods
2 green onions (with tops)
3 tablespoons vegetable oil
1 teaspoon finely chopped gingerroot
1 teaspoon finely chopped garlic
2 tablespoons vegetable oil
1/4 cup shredded canned bamboo shoots
2 teaspoons chili paste*
1/2 teaspoon sugar
1 1/4 cups chicken broth
1 tablespoon soy sauce

Soak mushrooms in warm water until soft, about 30 minutes; drain. Rinse in warm water; drain. Remove and discard stems; shred caps. Trim fat from beef; shred beef. Toss beef, 1 tablespoon vegetable oil, 1 teaspoon cornstarch, 1/2 teaspoon soy sauce and the white pepper in glass or plastic bowl. Cover and refrigerate 20 minutes. Soak noodles in cold water 5 minutes; drain.

Rinse bean sprouts in cold water; drain. Remove strings from pea pods. Place pea pods in boiling water. Cover and cook 1 minute; drain. Immediately rinse under running cold water; drain. Cut pea pods lengthwise into 1/4-inch strips. Cut green onions into 2-inch pieces.

Heat wok or 12-inch skillet until 1 or 2 drops of water bubble and skitter when sprinkled in wok. Add 3 tablespoons vegetable oil; rotate wok to coat side. Add beef, gingerroot and garlic; stir-fry until beef is brown, about 3 minutes. Remove beef from wok.

Add 2 tablespoons oil; rotate wok. Add mushrooms, bean sprouts, bamboo shoots, chili paste and sugar; stir-fry 1 minute. Stir in noodles, broth and soy sauce; heat to boiling. Cook and stir until noodles are tender, about 2 minutes. Stir in beef and pea pods; heat to boiling. Garnish with onions.

*1/2 teaspoon finely chopped dried chili pepper mixed with 1 tablespoon soy sauce can be substituted for the chili paste.

Beef Goulash

1½ pounds ground beef
1 medium onion, chopped
1 stalk celery, sliced
1 can (16 ounces) stewed tomatoes
1 tomato can water
1 package (7 ounces) uncooked elbow
    macaroni (2 cups)
1 can (6 ounces) tomato paste
1 tablespoon Worcestershire sauce
1 teaspoon salt
½ teaspoon pepper

Cook and stir ground beef, onion and celery in 4-quart ovenproof Dutch oven until beef is brown; drain. Stir in remaining ingredients.

Cover and bake in 350° oven until liquid is absorbed and goulash is hot, about 40 minutes; stir.

ITALIAN SAUSAGE GOULASH: Substitute 1½ pounds bulk Italian sausage for the ground beef. Omit salt and pepper.

Cincinnati-style Chili

1 pound ground beef
3 medium onions, chopped
1 tablespoon chili powder
1 teaspoon salt
1 can (16 ounces) whole tomatoes,
    undrained
1 can (15½ ounces) kidney beans,
    undrained
1 can (8 ounces) tomato sauce
1 package (6 or 7 ounces) uncooked
    spaghetti
1¼ cups shredded Cheddar cheese
    (5 ounces)

Cook and stir ground beef and about 1 cup of the onions in 3-quart saucepan until beef is brown and onions are tender; drain. Stir in chili powder, salt, tomatoes, beans and tomato sauce; break up tomatoes. Cook uncovered over medium heat until of desired consistency, about 10 minutes.

Cook spaghetti as directed on package; drain. For each serving, spoon about ¾ cup beef mixture over 1 cup hot spaghetti. Sprinkle each serving with ¼ cup cheese and about 2 tablespoons remaining onion.

Top with dollop of dairy sour cream and sliced hot chili, if desired.

Following pages: Stir-fried Noodles and Steak

Manicotti

1 pound ground beef
1 large onion, chopped (about 1 cup)
2 large cloves garlic, crushed
1 can (28 ounces) whole tomatoes
1 can (8 ounces) mushroom stems and pieces, drained
¼ cup snipped fresh parsley
1 teaspoon salt
1 teaspoon fennel seed
1 tablespoon snipped fresh basil leaves or 1 teaspoon dried basil leaves
2 packages (10 ounces each) frozen chopped spinach
2 cups creamed cottage cheese (small curd)
⅓ cup grated Parmesan cheese
¼ teaspoon ground nutmeg
¼ teaspoon pepper
14 uncooked manicotti shells
2 tablespoons grated Parmesan cheese

Cook and stir ground beef, onion and garlic in 10-inch skillet until beef is brown, about 10 minutes; drain. Stir in tomatoes (with liquid), mushrooms, parsley, salt, fennel seed and basil. Break up tomatoes with fork. Heat to boiling; reduce heat. Cover and simmer beef mixture 10 minutes.

Spoon about ⅓ of the beef mixture in ungreased rectangular baking dish, 13 × 9 × 2 inches. Rinse spinach under running cold water to separate; drain. Place spinach on towels and squeeze until dry. Mix spinach, cottage cheese, ⅓ cup Parmesan cheese, the nutmeg and pepper. Fill uncooked manicotti shells with spinach mixture; place shells on beef mixture in dish. Pour remaining beef mixture evenly over shells, covering shells completely; sprinkle with 2 tablespoons Parmesan cheese. Cover and cook in 350° oven until shells are tender, about 1½ hours.

Fettuccine with Pepperoni

1 package (16 ounces) fettuccine noodles
1 package (about 4 ounces) sliced pepperoni
1 can (8 ounces) mushroom stems and pieces, drained
2 tablespoons margarine or butter
¾ cup half-and-half
½ cup grated Parmesan cheese
1 tablespoon snipped fresh parsley

Cook fettuccine as directed on package; drain. Cut pepperoni slices into halves. Cook pepperoni in 2-quart saucepan over medium heat until light brown; drain and reserve. Cook mushrooms in margarine in same pan, stirring occasionally, until mushrooms are light brown. Stir in half-and-half and cheese; heat just until hot. Stir in reserved pepperoni and the parsley; toss with fettuccine. Serve with additional grated Parmesan cheese, if desired.

Stir-fried Pork and Pasta

6 SERVINGS

1¼ pounds pork boneless loin or leg
1 teaspoon cornstarch
1 teaspoon soy sauce
¼ teaspoon salt
⅛ teaspoon pepper
2 tablespoons vegetable oil
2 large cloves garlic, finely chopped
¼ to ½ teaspoon finely crushed dried red
    pepper
2 medium stalks celery, diagonally cut
    into ¼-inch slices (about 1 cup)
1 small green pepper, cut into 1-inch
    pieces
2 cups bean sprouts (about 4 ounces)
4 ounces mushrooms, sliced (about
    1¼ cups)
2 cups cooked vermicelli (about 4 ounces
    uncooked)
3 green onions (with tops), sliced
1 tablespoon soy sauce

Trim fat from pork. Cut pork into strips, 2 × 1 × ⅛ inch. Toss pork, cornstarch, 1 teaspoon soy sauce, the salt and pepper. Cover and refrigerate 20 minutes.

Heat oil in 12-inch skillet or wok over high heat until hot. Add pork, garlic and red pepper; cook and stir until pork is no longer pink, about 5 minutes. Add celery and green pepper; cook and stir 2 minutes. Add bean sprouts and mushrooms; cook and stir 2 minutes. Add vermicelli, green onions and 1 tablespoon soy sauce; toss until thoroughly mixed, about 2 minutes.

Mostaccioli with Prosciutto and Pine Nuts

4 SERVINGS

8 ounces uncooked mostaccioli (about
    3 cups)
1 bunch green onions (with tops), sliced
¼ cup pine nuts, pistachio nuts or sliv-
    ered almonds
½ teaspoon seasoned salt
⅓ cup margarine or butter
¼ pound prosciutto or thinly sliced fully
    cooked smoked ham, cut into thin
    strips
1 cup freshly grated Parmesan cheese

Cook mostaccioli as directed on package; drain. Cook and stir onions, pine nuts and seasoned salt in margarine in 10-inch skillet over medium heat until onions are tender, about 3 minutes.

Toss onion mixture, prosciutto, ½ cup of the cheese and the hot mostaccioli. Sprinkle with remaining cheese.

Following pages: Mostaccioli with Prosciutto and Pine Nuts

Green Lasagne with Two Sauces

Meat Sauce (below)
Green Noodles (below) or 12 spinach lasagne noodles, cooked and drained
Cheese Filling (page 67)
White Sauce (page 38)

Prepare Meat Sauce, Green Noodles, Cheese Filling and White Sauce. Reserve ½ cup of the Cheese Filling. Spread 1 cup of the Meat Sauce in ungreased oblong baking dish, 13½ × 9 × 2 inches. Layer 3 lasagne noodles, ½ of the White Sauce, ½ of the remaining Cheese Filling, 3 lasagne noodles and ½ of the remaining Meat Sauce; repeat. Sprinkle with reserved Cheese Filling. Cook uncovered in 350° oven until hot and bubbly, about 35 minutes. Let stand 10 minutes before cutting.

MEAT SAUCE

8 ounces bulk Italian sausage, crumbled
2 packages (2.5 ounces each) smoked sliced chicken or turkey, finely chopped
1 large onion, finely chopped
1 medium stalk celery, finely chopped
1 medium carrot, finely shredded
2 cloves garlic, finely chopped
1¾ cups water
¾ cup dry red wine
⅓ cup tomato paste
½ teaspoon Italian herb seasoning
⅛ teaspoon pepper
Dash of ground nutmeg

Cook and stir sausage until light brown; drain. Stir in remaining ingredients. Heat to boiling; reduce heat. Simmer uncovered, stirring occasionally, 1 hour.

GREEN NOODLES

Prepare dough for Green Fettuccine (page 82). After standing period, divide dough into halves. Roll one half into rectangle, 13 × 12 inches; cut rectangle into 6 strips, 13 × 2 inches each. Repeat with remaining dough. Spread strips on rack; let stand 30 minutes.

Heat water to rapid boiling; stir in 1 tablespoon salt, 1 tablespoon oil and the noodles. Cook uncovered over medium heat until nearly tender, 15 to 20 minutes. Drain; rinse with cold water. Place in single layer between sheets of waxed paper.

CHEESE FILLING

2 cups shredded mozzarella cheese
1½ cups grated Parmesan cheese
¼ cup snipped fresh parsley

Toss cheeses and parsley.

Austrian Ham-and-Noodle Casserole

4 SERVINGS

8 ounces uncooked wide egg noodles
¼ cup margarine or butter
1 medium onion, chopped
2 eggs, beaten
½ cup dairy sour cream
2 cups diced fully cooked smoked ham
*   (about ½ pound)*
½ teaspoon caraway seed, if desired
¼ teaspoon pepper
¼ cup dry bread crumbs
Paprika

Drop noodles into 6 cups rapidly boiling salted water (4 teaspoons salt). Heat to rapid boiling. Cook, stirring constantly, 3 minutes. Cover and remove from heat; let stand 10 minutes. Drain.

Stir margarine and onion into noodles. Stir eggs into sour cream. Stir egg mixture, ham, caraway seed and pepper into noodles. Sprinkle bread crumbs evenly in greased 2-quart casserole. Pour noodle mixture into casserole.

Sprinkle with paprika. Cook uncovered in 350° oven until mixture is set, 40 to 45 minutes.

Serve from casserole or unmold onto heated platter. To unmold, loosen edge of noodles around inside rim with knife. Place inverted platter over casserole; invert noodles onto platter. Garnish with parsley, if desired.

Pasta Shells in Bell Pepper Sauce

6 SERVINGS

3 red bell peppers, chopped
1 medium onion, chopped (about ½ cup)
1 clove garlic, finely chopped
2 tablespoons vegetable oil
1 teaspoon instant chicken bouillon
¼ teaspoon salt
¼ teaspoon ground red chilies
1 pound bulk chorizo sausage
2 cups whole kernel corn
6 ounces shredded Monterey Jack cheese
   (1½ cups)
5 ounces queso fresco or feta cheese,
   crumbled (about 1 cup)
1 egg
8 ounces uncooked jumbo pasta shells
1 jar (1 ounce) pine nuts (¼ cup), toasted

Cook and stir bell peppers, onion and garlic in oil in 10-inch skillet until tender. Stir in bouillon (dry), salt and ground red chilies. Heat to boiling; reduce heat. Cover and simmer 5 minutes.

Pour mixture into food processor workbowl fitted with steel blade or into blender container; cover and process until smooth. Pour into ungreased rectangular baking dish, $13 \times 9 \times 2$ inches.

Cook and stir sausage until brown; drain. Mix sausage, corn, cheeses and egg; reserve. Cook shells as directed on package; drain.

Heat oven to 350°. Fill each shell with about 2 tablespoons sausage mixture; place on sauce in baking dish. Cover and bake until hot, about 30 minutes. Sprinkle with pine nuts.

Ground Lamb Stroganoff

4 SERVINGS

1 pound ground lamb
1 medium onion, chopped
1 can (10¾ ounces) condensed cream of
   chicken soup
1 can (4 ounces) mushroom stems and
   pieces, drained
½ teaspoon seasoned salt
¼ teaspoon pepper
½ cup dairy sour cream or plain yogurt
Hot buttered spinach noodles
1 medium carrot, finely shredded

Cook and stir ground lamb and onion in 10-inch skillet until lamb is brown; drain. Stir in soup, mushrooms, seasoned salt and pepper. Heat to boiling; reduce heat. Simmer uncovered, stirring frequently, 5 minutes.

Stir in sour cream; heat just until hot. Serve over noodles; sprinkle with carrot.

GROUND BEEF STROGANOFF: Substitute 1 pound ground beef for the lamb.

· 7 ·

PASTA AS SALAD

Dilled Pasta Salad

½ cup mayonnaise or salad dressing
¼ cup dairy sour cream
1 tablespoon snipped fresh dill or ½ teaspoon dried dill weed
½ teaspoon salt
½ teaspoon dry mustard
¼ teaspoon pepper
2 cups spiral macaroni, cooked and drained
½ cup sliced ripe olives
1 medium zucchini, thinly sliced
1 medium carrot, coarsely shredded
1 small onion, chopped (about ¼ cup)

Mix mayonnaise, sour cream, dill, salt, mustard and pepper in 2½-quart bowl. Add remaining ingredients; toss. Cover and refrigerate at least 3 hours.

Pesto Salad

6 SERVINGS

3 cups uncooked medium shell macaroni
1 tablespoon olive or vegetable oil
1 cup Pesto Sauce (page 89) or
    commercially prepared pesto
4 Italian plum tomatoes, each cut into
    4 wedges
½ cup small pitted ripe olives
¼ cup white wine vinegar
4 cups coarsely shredded fresh spinach
Grated Parmesan cheese

Cook macaroni as directed on package; drain. Rinse in cold water; drain and toss with oil.

Mix Pesto Sauce, tomatoes, olives and vinegar in large bowl. Arrange 2 cups of the macaroni and 2 cups of the spinach on pesto mixture; repeat with remaining macaroni and spinach. Cover and refrigerate at least 2 hours but no longer than 24 hours. Toss; sprinkle with cheese.

PESTO AND SHRIMP SALAD: Add 1 package (6 ounces) frozen cooked tiny shrimp, thawed, just before tossing.

PESTO AND TUNA SALAD: Add 1 can (6½ ounces) tuna, drained, just before tossing.

Mediterranean Pasta Salad

8 SERVINGS

2 cups cooked small macaroni shells
2 medium tomatoes, chopped (about
    1½ cups)
1 small leek, thinly sliced (about ½ cup)
½ cup sliced ripe olives
2 tablespoons capers
½ cup mayonnaise or salad dressing
1 tablespoon lemon juice
1½ teaspoons snipped fresh basil leaves
    or ½ teaspoon dried basil leaves
½ teaspoon salt
1 large clove garlic, crushed
Dash of red pepper sauce
2 cups shredded lettuce

Mix macaroni, tomatoes, leek, olives and capers. Stir together mayonnaise, lemon juice, basil, salt, garlic and pepper sauce; toss with macaroni mixture until evenly coated. Cover and refrigerate at least 2 hours. Just before serving, toss macaroni mixture with lettuce.

Turkey-Pasta Salad

Spinach Sauce (below)
2 packages (5 ounces each) spiral
* macaroni*
3 cups cut-up cooked turkey or chicken
½ cup sliced ripe olives
1 tablespoon olive or vegetable oil
1 teaspoon vinegar
1 tablespoon pine nuts or slivered
* almonds*

SPINACH SAUCE

4 cups spinach leaves
1 cup parsley sprigs
¼ cup lemon juice
3 large cloves garlic, cut into halves
½ cup grated Parmesan cheese
2 tablespoons olive or vegetable oil
1 tablespoon snipped fresh basil leaves
* or 1 teaspoon dried basil leaves*
½ teaspoon pepper

Prepare Spinach Sauce. Cook macaroni as directed on package; drain. Rinse under running cold water; drain. Toss macaroni with ½ cup Spinach Sauce. Toss turkey, olives, oil and vinegar; spoon into center of macaroni mixture. Sprinkle with pine nuts. Serve with remaining Spinach Sauce.

Place half each of the spinach, parsley, lemon juice and garlic in blender container. Cover and blend on medium speed, stopping blender frequently to scrape sides, until spinach leaves are finely chopped, about 3 minutes. Repeat with remaining spinach, parsley, lemon juice and garlic. Place all spinach mixture in blender container. Add cheese, oil, basil and pepper. Cover and blend on medium speed, stopping blender frequently to scrape sides, until mixture is smooth, about 2 minutes.

Following pages: Muffuletta Salad, left (page 75), and Mediterranean Pasta Salad, right

Ham and Pasta Salad

Italian Dressing (below)
1 package (10 ounces) frozen chopped
    broccoli, cooked and drained
1 package (10 ounces) pasta bows
    (farfalle), cooked and drained
1 pound fully cooked smoked ham, cut
    into julienne strips
1 small green pepper, chopped (about
    ½ cup)
2 tablespoons finely chopped onion

Prepare Italian Dressing. Gently toss with remaining ingredients. Cover and refrigerate at least 6 hours.

ITALIAN DRESSING

¼ cup grated Parmesan cheese
¼ cup olive or vegetable oil
2 tablespoons snipped fresh parsley
2 tablespoons lemon juice
2 tablespoons vinegar
1 teaspoon dry mustard
1 tablespoon snipped fresh basil leaves
    or 1 teaspoon dried basil leaves
¾ teaspoon snipped fresh oregano leaves
    or ¼ teaspoon dried oregano leaves
¾ teaspoon snipped fresh marjoram
    leaves or ¼ teaspoon dried marjoram
    leaves
⅛ teaspoon pepper
1 medium clove garlic, crushed

Shake all ingredients in tightly covered jar.

Muffuletta Salad

Olive-Tomato Dressing (below)
2 cups uncooked mostaccioli
1 tablespoon olive oil
1/4 pound sliced salami, cut into 1/8-inch
   strips
1/4 pound thinly sliced fully cooked smoked
   ham, cut into 1/8-inch strips
1/4 pound provolone cheese, cut into
   1/8-inch strips
Salad greens

Prepare Olive-Tomato Dressing. Cook mostaccioli as directed on package; drain. Rinse in cold water; drain. Toss mostaccioli and oil.

Layer mostaccioli, salami, ham, provolone and salad greens on Olive-Tomato Dressing. Cover and refrigerate at least 4 hours but no longer than 24 hours. Toss just before serving. Arrange on salad greens.

OLIVE-TOMATO DRESSING

1 anchovy fillet, mashed
1 large clove garlic, crushed
1/3 cup olive oil
1 cup cherry tomatoes, cut into halves
1/2 cup chopped pimiento-stuffed olives
1/2 cup chopped Greek or ripe olives
1/2 cup chopped mixed pickled vegetables
1 1/2 teaspoons snipped fresh oregano
   leaves or 1/2 teaspoon dried oregano
   leaves

Stir anchovy and garlic thoroughly into oil in large bowl. Stir in remaining ingredients.

Seafood Salad with Ginger Dressing

6 SERVINGS

8 ounces uncooked vermicelli
Ginger Dressing (below)
2 cups bite-size pieces cooked seafood or
  1 package (8 ounces) frozen salad-
  style imitation crabmeat, thawed
½ cup coarsely chopped jícama or water
  chestnuts
¼ cup snipped fresh cilantro or parsley
2 medium carrots, shredded
1 medium cucumber, halved and sliced

Break vermicelli into halves. Cook as directed on package; drain. Rinse in cold water; drain.

Prepare Ginger Dressing. Toss dressing, vermicelli and remaining ingredients. Spoon onto salad greens, if desired.

GINGER DRESSING

⅓ cup mayonnaise or salad dressing
⅓ cup plain yogurt
1 tablespoon soy sauce
1 teaspoon sugar
½ teaspoon ground ginger
Dash of red pepper sauce, hot chili oil
  or hot sesame oil

Mix all ingredients in large bowl.

CHICKEN SALAD WITH GINGER DRESSING: Substitute 2 cups cut-up cooked chicken or turkey for the seafood.

Italian Tuna and Spiral Pasta Salad

4 SERVINGS

1 package (7 ounces) uncooked spiral
  macaroni (about 3 cups)
2 cans (6½ ounces each) tuna, chilled and
  drained
1 jar (6 ounces) marinated artichoke
  hearts, chilled and undrained
¼ cup Italian dressing
2 tablespoons snipped fresh parsley
2 tablespoons capers, drained
Dash of pepper

Cook macaroni as directed on package; drain. Rinse in cold water; drain. Mix macaroni and remaining ingredients. Serve on salad greens, if desired.

Tuna Toss

2 cans (6½ ounces each) tuna in water, drained
2 medium tomatoes, chopped (about 1½ cups)
2 cloves garlic, crushed
1 small onion, thinly sliced and separated into rings
½ cup pitted small ripe olives
2 tablespoons snipped fresh parsley
2 tablespoons olive or vegetable oil
½ teaspoon salt
1½ teaspoons snipped fresh basil leaves or ½ teaspoon dried basil leaves
¾ teaspoon snipped fresh oregano leaves or ¼ teaspoon dried oregano leaves
⅛ teaspoon coarsely ground pepper
2 cups uncooked pasta bows (farfalle)

Mix all ingredients except pasta bows. Cover and refrigerate at least 2 hours but no longer than 24 hours.

Cook bows as directed on package; drain. Immediately toss with tuna mixture. Serve salad on lettuce leaves and garnish with anchovies, if desired.

Shrimp and Macaroni Salad

1½ cups uncooked elbow or spiral macaroni (about 6 ounces)
1 package (10 ounces) frozen green peas
1 cup shredded Cheddar cheese (4 ounces)
¾ cup mayonnaise or salad dressing
½ cup sliced green onions (with tops)
⅓ cup sweet pickle relish
½ teaspoon salt
1 stalk celery, sliced (about ½ cup)
1 can (4½ ounces) tiny shrimp, rinsed and drained
½ head iceberg lettuce, torn into bite-size pieces (about 3 cups)
6 slices bacon, crisply cooked and crumbled

Cook macaroni as directed on package; drain. Rinse frozen peas under running cold water to separate; drain. Mix macaroni, peas and remaining ingredients except lettuce and bacon. Refrigerate until chilled, at least 4 hours.

Just before serving, toss macaroni mixture with lettuce and bacon.

CHEESE AND MACARONI SALAD: Omit shrimp. Increase cheese to 2 cups.

CHICKEN AND MACARONI SALAD: Substitute ½ cup cut-up cooked chicken or turkey for the canned shrimp.

HOMEMADE PASTA AND VERSATILE SAUCES

Spaetzle

ABOUT 3 CUPS COOKED SPAETZLE

2 eggs, beaten
1/4 cup milk or water
1 cup all-purpose flour
1/2 teaspoon salt
Dash of pepper
2 quarts water
1 teaspoon salt
2 tablespoons margarine or butter, melted

Mix eggs, milk, flour, 1/2 teaspoon salt and the pepper (batter will be thick). Heat water and 1 teaspoon salt to boiling in Dutch oven. Press batter through colander (preferably one with large holes), a few tablespoons at a time, into boiling water. Stir once or twice to prevent sticking. Cook until spaetzle rise to surface and are tender, about 5 minutes; drain. Pour margarine over spaetzle.

Egg Noodles

2 cups all-purpose flour
3 egg yolks
1 egg
2 teaspoons salt
¼ to ½ cup water

Make a well in center of flour. Add egg yolks, egg and salt; mix thoroughly. Mix in water, 1 tablespoon at a time, until dough is stiff but easy to roll. Divide dough into 4 equal parts. Roll one part at a time into paper-thin rectangle on generously floured cloth-covered board (keep remaining dough covered).

Loosely fold rectangle lengthwise into thirds; cut crosswise into ⅛-inch strips for narrow noodles, ¼-inch strips for wide noodles. Unfold strips and place on towels until stiff and dry, about 2 hours. Break strips into desired-size pieces.

Cook noodles in 3 quarts boiling salted water (1 tablespoon salt) until tender, 5 to 7 minutes; drain. (To cook half of the noodles, use 2 quarts water and 2 teaspoons salt.)

WHOLE WHEAT NOODLES: Substitute 2 cups whole wheat flour for all-purpose flour.

CORNMEAL NOODLES: Use 1½ cups all-purpose flour and ½ cup cornmeal in place of all-purpose flour.

FOOD PROCESSOR DIRECTIONS: Place flour, egg yolks, egg, salt and ¼ cup of the water in workbowl fitted with steel blade. Cover and process until mixture is moist and crumbly, about 10 seconds. Add remaining water, if necessary, by tablespoons; cover and process until dough forms a ball, 10 to 15 seconds longer. (Do not add any more water than necessary.) Continue as directed above.

Following pages: Egg noodles shown with Vegetable and Goat Cheese Sauce (page 96)

Green Fettuccine

8 ounces fresh spinach*
2 eggs
1 tablespoon olive or vegetable oil
1 teaspoon salt
2 cups all-purpose flour
4½ quarts water
1 tablespoon salt
1 tablespoon olive or vegetable oil

Wash spinach; drain. Cover and cook over medium heat with just the water that clings to the leaves, 3 to 10 minutes. Rinse spinach under running cold water; drain well. Place spinach, eggs, 1 tablespoon oil and 1 teaspoon salt in blender container. Cover and blend on medium speed until smooth, about 20 seconds.

Make a well in center of flour. Add spinach mixture; mix thoroughly. (If dough is too dry, mix in a few drops water; if dough is too sticky, mix in small amount flour.) Gather dough into ball. Knead on lightly floured cloth-covered board until smooth and elastic, about 5 minutes. Let stand 10 minutes.

Divide dough into 4 equal parts. Roll one part at a time into paper-thin rectangle on generously floured cloth-covered board with cloth-covered rolling pin (keep remaining dough covered). Loosely fold rectangle lengthwise into thirds; cut crosswise into ¼-inch strips. Unfold strips and place on towel until dry, at least 30 minutes.

Heat water to boiling; stir in 1 tablespoon salt, 1 tablespoon oil and the noodles. Cook until almost tender, 3 to 5 minutes; drain.

FOOD PROCESSOR DIRECTIONS: Place cooked spinach, eggs, 1 tablespoon oil and 1 teaspoon salt in workbowl fitted with steel blade. Cover and process until smooth, about 15 seconds. Continue as directed above.

*1 package (10 ounces) frozen spinach can be substituted for the fresh spinach. Cook as directed on package; drain well.

Chipotle Fettuccine

2 cups all-purpose flour
½ teaspoon salt
1 tablespoon vegetable oil
2 eggs
1 to 2 canned chipotle chilies in adobo
  sauce, finely chopped

Mix flour and salt in large bowl; make well in center. Beat oil, eggs and chilies; pour into well. Stir with fork, gradually bringing flour mixture to center, until dough forms and rounds into a ball. If dough is too dry, mix in up to 2 tablespoons water. Roll and cut as directed below. (Use additional flour when rolling and cutting noodles.) Place fettuccine strips on towels; let stand 30 minutes.

Break fettuccine into desired-size pieces. Cook in 3 quarts boiling salted water (1 tablespoon salt) until tender, 8 to 10 minutes; drain.

HAND ROLLING METHOD: Knead dough on lightly floured surface until smooth and elastic, about 5 minutes. Divide into 4 equal parts. Roll dough, 1 part at a time, into paper-thin rectangle, about 14 × 10 inches (keep remaining dough covered). Loosely fold rectangle lengthwise into thirds; cut crosswise into ¼-inch strips. Unfold, and separate strips.

MANUAL PASTA MACHINE METHOD: Divide dough into 4 equal parts. Feed dough, 1 part at a time, through smooth rollers set at widest setting (keep remaining dough covered). Sprinkle with flour if dough becomes sticky. Fold lengthwise into thirds. Repeat feeding dough through rollers and folding into thirds until dough is firm and smooth, 8 to 10 times. Feed dough through progressively narrower settings until dough is paper thin. (Dough will lengthen as it becomes thinner; it may be cut crosswise at any time for easier handling.) Feed through fettuccine-cutting rollers.

Ravioli in Tomato Sauce

Ravioli Dough (page 85)
¾ pound ground beef
1 small onion, finely chopped
1 package (10 ounces) frozen chopped
  spinach, thawed and well drained
1 egg
½ cup grated Parmesan cheese
1 teaspoon salt
¼ teaspoon pepper

Prepare Ravioli Dough. While dough is resting, cook and stir ground beef and onion over medium heat until beef is light brown and finely crumbled; drain. Squeeze any remaining moisture from spinach. Stir spinach, egg, cheese, 1 teaspoon salt and the pepper into beef and onion.

Divide dough into 6 equal parts. (Cover dough with plastic wrap to prevent drying.) Roll one part of the dough as thin as possible on lightly floured surface into about 13-inch square. Trim edges to make 12-inch square; fold in half. (Cover with plastic wrap.) Repeat with a second part of dough, but do not fold.

Mound about 1 teaspoon beef filling about 1½ inches apart in checkerboard pattern on sheet of dough. Dip pastry brush into water; brush in straight lines between filling mounds and around edge of dough. Unfold folded sheet of dough over filled half. Starting at center, press with fingertips and side of hand around filling and edges to seal. Cut pasta between mounds into squares with pastry wheel or knife. Separate squares; place on waxed paper. Repeat twice with remaining dough to make 48 squares.

Heat water and 2 tablespoons salt to boiling in large kettle. Add ravioli; stir to prevent sticking. Cook uncovered until tender, about 12 minutes; remove to colander with slotted spoon. Serve with Tomato Sauce (page 88).

RAVIOLI DOUGH

3 cups all-purpose flour
3 egg yolks
3 eggs
1 tablespoon salt
¼ to ½ cup water

Make a well in center of flour. Add egg yolks, eggs and salt; mix thoroughly with fork. Mix in water, 1 tablespoon at a time, until dough forms a ball. Turn dough onto well-floured cloth-covered board; knead until smooth and elastic, about 5 minutes. Cover; let rest 10 minutes.

Do-Ahead Tip: After cutting ravioli into squares, place in single layer on cookie sheets; freeze. Place frozen ravioli in freezer containers; freeze no longer than 2 weeks. Cook frozen ravioli as directed above, about 15 minutes.

RAVIOLI IN CHEESE SAUCE: 1 cup margarine or butter, melted, and ½ cup grated Parmesan cheese can be substituted for the Tomato Sauce; toss with ravioli.

Following pages: Ravioli in Tomato Sauce

Tomato Sauce

ABOUT 2¼ CUPS SAUCE

2 cans (16 ounces each) tomatoes
1 can (15 ounces) tomato sauce
1 large onion, chopped
2 cloves garlic, chopped
2 teaspoons sugar
1 tablespoon snipped fresh basil leaves
  or 1 teaspoon dried basil leaves
½ teaspoon salt
¼ teaspoon pepper

Break up tomatoes with fork. Heat tomatoes (with liquid) and remaining ingredients to boiling; reduce heat. Simmer uncovered until thickened, about 30 minutes.

Vegetable-Basil Sauce

ABOUT 3½ CUPS SAUCE

¾ cup chopped onion (about 1 medium)
2 cloves garlic, crushed
3 tablespoons vegetable oil
6 cups chopped tomatoes (6 medium)
¾ cup dry red wine
⅓ cup snipped parsley
⅓ cup snipped fresh basil
1½ teaspoons sugar
1 to 1½ teaspoons salt
1 cup sliced zucchini
1 cup sliced fresh mushrooms
½ cup jumbo pitted ripe olive halves

Cook and stir onion and garlic in oil in Dutch oven over medium heat until onion is tender; stir in tomatoes, red wine, parsley, basil, sugar and salt.

Heat to boiling; reduce heat. Simmer uncovered, stirring frequently, until sauce is almost thickened, about 1 hour.

Add zucchini and mushrooms; cook until sauce is thickened, about 15 minutes longer. Stir in olives; heat thoroughly.

Pesto Sauce

2 cups firmly packed fresh basil leaves
¾ cup grated Parmesan cheese
¾ cup olive oil
2 tablespoons pine nuts
4 cloves garlic

Place all ingredients in blender container. Cover and blend on medium speed, stopping blender occasionally to scrape sides, until smooth, about 3 minutes.

Note: Pesto Sauce can be frozen no longer than 6 months. Let stand at room temperature until thawed, at least 4 hours. Toss with hot cooked pasta.

Eggplant-Tomato Sauce

1 medium eggplant, cut into ½-inch
* cubes*
2 medium onions, sliced
2 cloves garlic, finely chopped
¼ cup olive or vegetable oil
1 can (28 ounces) pear-shaped tomatoes,
* Italian-style*
1 can (15 ounces) tomato sauce
1 can (8 ounces) mushroom stems and
* pieces, drained*
½ cup grated Parmesan cheese
1 tablespoon sugar
1 teaspoon salt
3 teaspoons snipped fresh oregano leaves
* or 1 teaspoon dried oregano leaves*
3 teaspoons snipped fresh basil leaves or
* 1 teaspoon dried basil leaves*

Cook and stir eggplant, onions and garlic in oil in 4-quart Dutch oven until eggplant is tender, about 10 minutes. Stir in tomatoes (with liquid), tomato sauce, mushrooms, ½ cup cheese, the sugar, salt, oregano and basil; break up tomatoes with fork. Heat to boiling; reduce heat. Cover and simmer, stirring occasionally, 45 minutes.

Chicken-Tomato Sauce

ABOUT 3 CUPS SAUCE

1 cup water
1 teaspoon salt
1 teaspoon sugar
*1 tablespoon snipped fresh oregano leaves
or 1 teaspoon dried oregano leaves*
*2 teaspoons snipped fresh basil leaves or
3/4 teaspoon dried basil leaves*
*1 teaspoon snipped fresh marjoram leaves
or 1/2 teaspoon dried marjoram leaves*
*1/2 teaspoon snipped fresh rosemary leaves
or 1/4 teaspoon dried rosemary leaves,
if desired*
1 large onion, chopped
1 clove garlic, crushed
1 bay leaf
1 can (8 ounces) tomato sauce
1 can (6 ounces) tomato paste
1 1/2 cups cut-up cooked chicken

Heat all ingredients except chicken to boiling in 10-inch skillet; reduce heat. Cover and simmer 30 minutes, stirring occasionally.

Stir in chicken. Cover and simmer 30 minutes, stirring occasionally. Remove bay leaf. Serve over cooked spaghetti or other cooked pasta.

Amatriciana Sauce

ABOUT 2 1/4 CUPS SAUCE

1/4 pound salt pork
1 medium onion, chopped
1 clove garlic, chopped
1 tablespoon olive or vegetable oil
1 can (28 ounces) tomatoes
1 teaspoon sugar
1/4 to 1/2 teaspoon pepper

Trim rind from salt pork; dice pork. Cook and stir salt pork, onion and garlic in oil in 10-inch skillet until onion is tender; drain. Add tomatoes (with liquid), sugar and pepper; break up tomatoes with fork. Simmer uncovered until mixture is desired consistency, 30 to 40 minutes.

Meatballs in Tomato Sauce

20 MEATBALLS WITH ABOUT 3½ CUPS SAUCE

1 large onion, chopped (about 1 cup)
1 clove garlic, crushed
1 teaspoon sugar
*1 tablespoon snipped fresh oregano leaves
   or 1 teaspoon dried oregano leaves*
¾ teaspoon salt
*2 teaspoons snipped fresh basil leaves or
   ¾ teaspoon dried basil leaves*
*1½ teaspoons snipped fresh marjoram
   leaves or ½ teaspoon dried marjoram leaves*
*1 can (16 ounces) whole tomatoes,
   undrained*
1 can (8 ounces) tomato sauce
Meatballs (below)

Mix all ingredients except Meatballs in 3-quart saucepan; break up tomatoes. Heat to boiling; reduce heat. Cover and simmer, stirring occasionally, 30 minutes.

Prepare Meatballs; drain. Stir Meatballs into tomato mixture. Cover and simmer, stirring occasionally, 30 minutes longer.

MEATBALLS

1 pound ground beef
½ cup dry bread crumbs
¼ cup milk
¾ teaspoon salt
½ teaspoon Worcestershire sauce
¼ teaspoon pepper
1 small onion, chopped (about ¼ cup)
1 egg

Heat oven to 400°. Mix all ingredients; shape into twenty 1½-inch balls. Place in ungreased rectangular pan, 13 × 9 × 2 inches. Bake uncovered until done and light brown, 20 to 25 minutes.

Following pages: Cornmeal Noodles (page 79), shown with Chicken-Tomato Sauce

Ground Beef in Tomato Sauce

1 pound ground beef
1 large onion, chopped (about 1 cup)
1 clove garlic, crushed
1 teaspoon sugar
1 tablespoon snipped fresh oregano leaves
   or 1 teaspoon dried oregano leaves
¾ teaspoon salt
2 teaspoons snipped fresh basil leaves or
   ¾ teaspoon dried basil leaves
1½ teaspoons snipped fresh marjoram
   leaves or ½ teaspoon dried marjo-
   ram leaves
1 can (16 ounces) whole tomatoes,
   undrained
1 can (8 ounces) tomato sauce

Cook and stir ground beef, onion and garlic in 10-inch skillet until beef is light brown; drain. Stir in remaining ingredients; break up tomatoes. Heat to boiling; reduce heat. Cover and simmer, stirring occasionally, 1 hour.

Ground Beef in Red Wine Sauce

ABOUT 6 CUPS SAUCE

1½ pounds ground beef
½ cup finely chopped onion
2 cloves garlic, finely chopped
¼ cup olive oil
½ cup chopped green bell pepper
¼ cup snipped fresh parsley
1 tablespoon snipped fresh basil leaves
  or ¾ teaspoon dried basil leaves
2 teaspoons snipped fresh oregano leaves
  or ½ teaspoon dried oregano leaves
1½ teaspoons salt
½ teaspoon pepper
¼ teaspoon sugar
3 cans (8 ounces each) tomato sauce
1 can (4 ounces) mushroom stems and
  pieces, undrained
1 cup zinfandel or dry red wine

Cook and stir ground beef, onion and garlic in oil in 4-quart Dutch oven until beef is brown; drain. Stir in remaining ingredients except wine. Heat to boiling; reduce heat. Cover and simmer 1 hour, stirring occasionally.

Stir in wine. Cover and simmer 30 minutes, stirring occasionally. Uncover and simmer 30 minutes longer, stirring occasionally.

Beef and Prosciutto Sauce

ABOUT 6 CUPS SAUCE

1 pound ground beef
2 medium onions, sliced
2 cloves garlic, finely chopped
1 can (28 ounces) tomatoes
¼ pound prosciutto,* cut into thin strips
¾ cup dry red wine
1 teaspoon sugar
½ teaspoon salt
1½ teaspoons snipped fresh rosemary
  leaves or ½ teaspoon dried rosemary
  leaves, crushed
¼ teaspoon ground nutmeg
¼ teaspoon pepper

Cook and stir beef, onions and garlic in 10-inch skillet until beef is light brown; drain. Stir in tomatoes (with liquid) and remaining ingredients; break up tomatoes with fork. Cover and simmer 15 minutes, stirring occasionally. Uncover and simmer, stirring occasionally, about 1 hour.

*Dried beef can be substituted for the prosciutto.

Vegetable and Goat Cheese Sauce

ABOUT 5 CUPS SAUCE

1 tablespoon all-purpose flour
1 tablespoon instant chicken bouillon
1 tablespoon snipped fresh marjoram
    leaves or 1 teaspoon dried marjo-
    ram leaves
1/2 teaspoon salt
1/4 teaspoon white pepper
1 1/4 cups water
8 ounces goat cheese, cut into 1/2-inch
    cubes
2 1/2 cups broccoli flowerets, cut into
    1 1/4-inch pieces
2 1/2 cups cauliflowerets, cut into 1 1/4-inch
    pieces
3/4 cup 1 × 1/4 × 1/8-inch carrot strips
3 tablespoons chopped green onion

Mix flour, bouillon (dry), marjoram, salt and white pepper in saucepan; gradually stir in water. Heat to boiling, stirring constantly. Boil and stir 1 minute; reduce heat to simmer. Stir in cheese. Cook and stir until melted, 3 to 5 minutes; keep warm.

Place steamer basket in 1/2 inch water in saucepan or skillet (water should not touch bottom of basket). Place broccoli, cauliflower and carrots in basket. Cover tightly and heat to boiling; reduce heat. Steam until vegetables are crisp-tender, about 4 minutes.

Stir vegetables and onion into cheese sauce.

White Clam Sauce

ABOUT 3 CUPS SAUCE

1 medium onion, chopped
1 clove garlic, finely chopped
3 tablespoons margarine or butter
1 tablespoon all-purpose flour
3 cans (6 1/2 ounces each) minced clams
1/2 teaspoon salt
1 1/2 teaspoons snipped fresh basil leaves
    or 1/2 teaspoon dried basil leaves
1/8 teaspoon pepper
1/4 cup snipped fresh parsley

Cook and stir onion and garlic in margarine in 2-quart saucepan until onion is tender; stir in flour. Add clams (with liquid), salt, basil and pepper. Heat to boiling; reduce heat. Cover and simmer 5 minutes. Stir in parsley.

RED SPOON TIPS

Cooking Pasta Perfectly

Whether you purchase commercially made fresh or dried pasta or make your pasta yourself, ultimate success boils down to one thing: If pasta is not properly cooked, the resulting dish won't be as good as it could be. It was common in this country to boil pasta until it was soft. Today, more people have discovered that they like their pasta as the Italians prefer it, *al dente* (literally "to the tooth," meaning tender but firm). Because mushy pasta loses much of its flavor and character, taste pasta before the recommended cooking time is up. That way, you can stop cooking it just when it reaches the stage you like best.

Some cooks advise adding oil to the cooking water to keep pasta from sticking—to itself and to the pot. When pasta sticks, it's usually because the water stopped boiling when the pasta was added. It isn't necessary to add oil. Just be sure that the water is at a rapid, rolling boil when you add the pasta, that you add it so the boiling doesn't stop, and that there is enough water to begin with. How much water is enough? About 3 quarts of water are needed for every 8 ounces of pasta. You can simply fill your largest pot. When the water comes to a boil, add a good pinch of salt if you like; let the water return to a rolling boil before adding pasta.

Some dried pasta shapes are too large to be submerged all at once. Place one end of lasagne, spaghetti or other long pasta in the water; as it softens, gently push it down into the water.

PASTA YIELDS

UNCOOKED PASTA	COOKED PASTA	
	CUPS	SERVINGS
Macaroni		
6–7 ounces (2 cups)	4	4–6
Spaghetti		
7–8 ounces	4	4–6
Noodles		
8 ounces	4–5	4–6
Homemade pasta		
12–14 ounces	4	4–6

Pasta Identification by Shape

The many varieties of pasta on the market offer a fascinating assortment of sizes and shapes. Some shapes are known by more than one name. You can often determine size of pasta from the Italian suffix—"oni" means the pasta is large, and "elle," "ina," "ini" and "iti" mean the pasta is small.

PASTA DESCRIPTION AND USE

SPECIFIC NAME	SHAPE	DESCRIPTION	USE
MACARONI			
Alphabets		tiny pasta alphabet	soups
Anelli		tiny pasta rings	soups
Conchiglie		smooth or ridged shell-shaped pasta in several sizes	soups or stuffed
Ditali		large pasta "thimbles" with ridges	casseroles, salads, soups or with sauces
Elbow macaroni		curved tubes in a variety of sizes and lengths	casseroles, soups
Farfalle		pasta shaped like bows in a variety of sizes and colors	soups, stuffings
Lumache		small- to medium-size snail-shaped pasta	casseroles, salads or with sauces
Macaroni		pasta tubes in a variety of sizes and shapes	casseroles or soups
Mostaccioli		medium-size pasta tubes with diagonally cut ends	served with hearty meat or tomato sauce

Specific Name	Shape	Description	Use
Orzo		tiny pasta resembling oats	soups or cooked like rice
Rigatoni		slightly curved small tubes	casseroles or soups
Risini		tiny rice-shaped pasta	soups
Ziti		short, smooth tubes	casseroles

NOODLES

Fettuccine		about ¼-inch-wide ribbon noodles, straight or in coils	buttered or in rich meat sauce
Lasagne		wide pasta, sometimes with curly edges	baked dishes
Noodle flakes		very fine egg pasta sheets cut into ¼-inch squares	soups
Tagliatelle		¾-inch-wide egg noodles	casseroles or with sauces

SPAGHETTI

Bucatini		typical spaghetti but hollow instead of solid	with sauces
Capellini		thin, often coiled, spaghetti	with sauces
Fusilli		strands of spiral-shaped pasta	with sauces
Linguine		flat, narrow, long	casseroles or with sauces
Spaghettini		long, fine-cut strands of spaghetti	with sauces

Specific Name	Shape	Description	Use
Vermicelli		straight or folded strands of very thin spaghetti	with sauces

MISCELLANEOUS PASTA

Cannelloni		4- to 6-inch pieces of large, fresh pasta rolled around a filling	baked with sauces
Manicotti		large smooth or ridged pasta tubes	cooked, filled with cheese or meat and baked
Ravioli		pasta dumpling filled with spinach and ricotta cheese or meat and herbs	served with sauce
Won ton skins		thin soft squares of noodle dough wrapped around or folded over filling of meat, vegetables or seafood	deep-fried, boiled or steamed

OTHER

Cellophane noodles		hard, clear white noodles made from mung beans; turn translucent when cooked in liquid, puffy and crisp when deep-fat fried	Oriental-style dishes
Rice sticks		thin, brittle white noodles made from rice powder	softened in liquid, then stir-fried or deep-fat fried in Oriental-style dishes

Source: General Mills, Inc.

Flavored Pastas

Today it is almost commonplace to see pasta flavored and colored with carrot, beet, spinach, artichoke, tomato paste, squid ink, various hot peppers, pumpkin and other squash. Of these, the spinach pasta probably has the most pronounced flavor. Flavored pastas can be pretty; give some thought to marrying the colors of the pasta and the sauce.

Making Pasta at Home

- If the pasta dough seems dry, drizzle in a little water and work it into the dough.
- If the dough is sticky, dust your hands and the countertop with flour. Knead flour gradually into the dough until it has the proper consistency.
- During kneading, bits of dry dough may flake off the dough mass. Don't try to knead them into the rest of the dough. They are too dry to be incorporated properly.
- If dough becomes sticky while you are cutting it into shapes, sprinkle the knife (or, if you are using a pasta machine, the rollers) and the surface of the dough with flour.

Serving Pasta

Pasta should be drained quickly and served as soon as possible after it has been cooked. Toss it with a little butter or olive or vegetable oil if the sauce isn't ready to add immediately. Serve pasta in warmed serving dishes. Most pasta dishes (with the exception of soups) can be eaten from plates. For many of the saucier dishes, a shallow soup bowl would be welcome.

Grated cheese doesn't automatically go with every Italian pasta dish. Traditionally it is not sprinkled over those already made with cheese or with game, fish or hot peppers.

Sauces

Tomato sauces were among the first Italian pasta sauces to catch America's fancy, followed by simple creamy Alfredo-type sauces. Now we enjoy a vast array of sauces, flavored with everything from gingerroot and soy sauce to sage, hot peppers, smoked fish and simple, good-quality olive oil. Sauces made without eggs, cheese or cream can be made ahead and frozen for later use. Let the sauce come to room temperature, then cover it tightly, label and freeze.

Kitchen Equipment

CHEESE GRATER: A four-sided standing grater is a good tool for grating such hard cheeses as Parmesan, but using it usually means standing at the kitchen counter with tiny shards of cheese flying. Hand-held cheese graters can do double service, in the kitchen and at the table, too. They are lightweight and can be adjusted to coarse, medium and fine grating.

COLLANDER: Unless you have a pasta pot with a wire insert, you'll need a collander to drain cooked pasta. Look for a large one that sits sturdily on three feet.

DRYING RACK: Homemade pasta should air-dry for at least thirty minutes before cooking. Many cooks think it dries best off the countertop so that air can circulate around it, and wire or wooden dowel racks do the trick. To dry long pasta strands without a rack, drape them over a broom handle set across the backs of two chairs.

ELECTRIC MIXER: Pasta dough can be mixed using the dough hook attachment. Add water just until the dough begins to hold together. The mixer will do much of the kneading for you; finish kneading by hand until the consistency feels correct.

FOOD PROCESSOR: Like an electric mixer, this machine will not only mix the dough but also do most of the kneading. Mixing by food processor seems to work best with all-purpose and durum flour, rather than the coarser flours. Use the metal blade. You will know that enough water or other liquid has been added when the dough begins to form a ball and the machine slows down. Finish kneading by hand until the proper consistency.

KNIFE: A good, sharp knife can take the place of a pasta-cutting wheel.

PASTA-CUTTING WHEEL (PIZZA OR PASTRY WHEEL): This little wheel makes cutting free-hand somewhat easier than using a knife. It's especially quick when used to navigate between rows of ravioli or cut lengths of pasta for lasagne.

PASTA MACHINE: This machine, available in electric or manual models, rolls pasta dough into sheets of uniform, desired thickness, then cuts the sheets into a wide variety of shapes. The manual version attaches to a countertop or table by means of a vise grip.

PASTA POT: An 8-quart pot is ideal. There are pots made especially for cooking pasta, fitted with a deep wire basket. When the pasta is cooked, simply lift the basket of pasta out of the boiling water; this avoids the balancing act over the sink with a collander and a heavy pot of scalding water. If you don't have a pasta pot, a large wire strainer can be used the same way.

RAVIOLI ROLLING PIN: This rolling pin has a raised grid. As the pin is rolled over the double layer of dough and filling, it marks and cuts out the ravioli. The edges have to be carefully sealed by hand.

RAVIOLI STAMP: Ravioli can be formed one at a time with this tool, which works like a cookie cutter. Placed over two sheets of dough with filling between, one movement cuts out the shape and seals the edges.

RAVIOLI TRAY (RAVIOLI PLAQUE): This looks like a shallow ice cube tray. Ravioli can be made by laying sheets of dough flat on a kitchen surface and dropping the filling in rows. Some prefer to use these trays for results of uniform size. The dough is draped on the tray, the filling dropped into the indentations and covered with another sheet of dough. The ravioli are separated freehand or by using a wheel.

ROLLING PIN: Use a solid rolling pin to roll out pasta dough. If you can find one that is especially long and narrow, it will make rolling wide sheets of dough easier.

SPAGHETTI RAKE: This wooden tool looks like a spoon with a grid of pegs coming out of one side. It is useful for catching lengths of pasta to taste them for doneness.

Pasta Cooking Timetable

Fresh Homemade Pasta	Cooking Time
Fettuccine	5 to 7 minutes
Lasagne	15 to 20 minutes
Noodles	5 to 7 minutes
Ravioli	12 to 14 minutes
Tortellini	25 to 30 minutes

Cooked dried homemade pasta a few minutes longer than fresh.

Dried Packaged Pasta		Cooking Time
Alphabets		4 to 5 minutes
Anelli		9 to 10 minutes
Ditalini		8 to 9 minutes
Elbow Macaroni		8 to 10 minutes
Farfalle		11 to 12 minutes
Fettuccine		10 to 12 minutes
Lasagne		10 to 12 minutes
Linguine		8 to 10 minutes
Manicotti		10 to 12 minutes
Mostaccioli		12 to 14 minutes
Noodles		6 to 8 minutes
Orzo or Rosamarina		5 to 8 minutes
Rigatoni		14 to 16 minutes
Rotini		10 to 12 minutes
Shell Macaroni	Small	6 to 8 minutes
	Medium	10 to 12 minutes
	Jumbo	12 to 15 minutes
Spaghetti		8 to 10 minutes
Tortellini		25 to 30 minutes
Vermicelli		4 to 6 minutes
Ziti		12 to 14 minutes

Seasonal Pasta Menus

In Italy, pasta is almost always a prelude to the main course. Here, and especially with the current interest in lighter eating, we have grown accustomed to thinking of it as the star attraction. For a heartier menu, follow the pasta course with whatever main dish may take your fancy. A juicy roast, accompanied by a selection of seasonal vegetables, would fill the bill with brio.

SPRING

Sliced cantaloupe or honeydew melon with lime
Mediterranean Pasta Salad (page 70)
Italian bread
Flan, crème brulée or baked custards
OR
Salad of Boston lettuce with fresh herbs and Feta cheese
Egg Noodles (page 79) with Vegetable-Basil Sauce (page 88)
Sesame bread sticks
Sliced fresh fruit in meringue shells with raspberry sauce

SUMMER

Cold consommé and cheese straws
Vermicelli with Lemony Green Vegetables (page 31)
Angel food cake with sliced strawberries
OR
Asparagus vinaigrette
Cornmeal Noodles (page 79) with Eggplant-Tomato Sauce (page 89)
Sorbet or ice cream with crisp wafer cookies

AUTUMN

Mostaccioli with Prosciutto and Pine Nuts (page 63)
Romaine and bell pepper salad
Crusty garlic bread
Hot apple crisp with maple nut ice cream
OR

Winter squash soup
Chipotle Fettuccine with Smoked Turkey in Corn Sauce (page 56)
Pecan pie or plum tart

WINTER

Black bean soup
Southwest Sautéed Scallops (page 40)
Corn sticks
Sliced oranges
OR
Salad of radicchio and endive
Rigatoni with Ground Beef in Red Wine Sauce (page 95)
Crusty bread
Devil's food cake with fudge frosting

All-Time Favorites Pasta Recipes

EXTRA SPECIAL

- Chicken Soup with Tortellini
- Vermicelli with Lemony Green Vegetables
- Fettuccine with Four Cheeses
- Scallops in Cream Sauce
- Chipotle Fettuccine with Smoked Turkey in Corn Sauce
- Ground Lamb Stroganoff
- Austrian Ham-and-Noodle Casserole
- Stir-fried Pork and Pasta

PREPARE EARLY, ENJOY FOR DINNER

- Italian Vegetable Soup
- Chunky Beef Noodle Soup
- Cheese Lasagne
- Macaroni with Marinated Tomatoes
- Green Lasagne with Two Sauces
- Zucchini Lasagne
- Vegetable Lasagne
- Seafood Lasagne
- Manicotti
- Ham and Pasta Salad
- Muffuletta Salad
- Shrimp and Macaroni Salad

JUST A FEW INGREDIENTS

- Oriental-style Chicken Noodle Soup
- Spaghetti alla Carbonara
- Rotini with Havarti and Herbs
- Double Cheese Tortellini
- Vermicelli with Smoked Fish and Gruyère
- Fettuccine with Pepperoni
- Mostaccioli with Prosciutto and Pine Nuts

ANY QUESTIONS?

How nutritious is pasta ... how is it produced? For answers to these and other questions, write for a copy of the Pasta Sourcebook (Published by the Nat'l Pasta Assoc.), 40 West 57th Street, Suite 1400, New York, NY 10019. Send $1.00 for postage and handling.

INDEX

V.P., Publisher: Anne M. Zeman
Project Editor: Rebecca W. Atwater
Editorial Assistant: Rachel A. Simon
Photographer: Anthony Johnson
Food Stylist: Paul Grimes
Designers: Patricia Fabricant, Frederick J. Latasa
Production Manager: Lessley Davis
Production Editor: Kimberly Ebert